THE WOODS ARE ON FIRE

TED KOOSER CONTEMPORARY POETRY | *Editor:* Ted Kooser

THE WOODS ARE ON FIRE

NEW AND SELECTED POEMS

FLEDA BROWN | Introduction by Ted Kooser

University of Nebraska Press | Lincoln & London

© 2017 by the Board of Regents of the
University of Nebraska

Acknowledgments for the use of copyrighted
material appear on pages xiii–xv, which
constitute an extension of the copyright page.

Publication of this volume was made possible
in part by the generous support of the
H. Lee and Carol Gendler Charitable Fund.

Library of Congress Cataloging-in-Publication Data
Names: Brown, Fleda, 1944– author. |
Kooser, Ted, writer of introduction.
Title: The woods are on fire: new and selected poems /
Fleda Brown; introduction by Ted Kooser.
Description: Lincoln: University of Nebraska Press,
[2017] | Series: Ted Kooser Contemporary Poetry
Identifiers: LCCN 2016034781 (print)
LCCN 2016041721 (ebook)
ISBN 9780803294943 (softcover: acid-free paper)
ISBN 9781496200327 (epub)
ISBN 9781496200334 (mobi)
ISBN 9781496200341 (pdf)
Classification: LCC PS3560.A21534 A6 2017 (print) |
LCC PS3560.A21534 (ebook) | DDC 811/.54—dc23
LC record available at https://lccn.loc.gov/2016034781

Designed and set in Fournier MT Pro by L. Auten.

All things, oh priests, are on fire . . . The eye is on fire; forms are on fire; eye-consciousness is on fire; impressions received by the eye are on fire.

THE BUDDHA

CONTENTS

ACKNOWLEDGMENTS

Poems selected from *Fishing with Blood* and *Do Not Peel the Birches* are reprinted by permission of Purdue University Press.

Poems selected from *Breathing In, Breathing Out* are reprinted by permission of Anhinga Press.

Poems selected *The Women Who Loved Elvis All Their Lives* © 2004 by Fleda Brown. Used by the permission of The Permission Company, Inc., on behalf of Carnegie Mellon University Press, www.cmu.edu /universitypress.

Poems selected from *Loon Cry: New and Selected Michigan Poems* are reprinted by permission of the author.

Poems selected from *Reunion* © 2007 by the Board of Regents of the University of Wisconsin System. Reprinted by permission of the University of Wisconsin Press.

Poems selected from *No Need of Sympathy* © 2013 by Fleda Brown. Used by the permission of The Permissions Company, Inc., on behalf of BOA Editions, Ltd., www.boaeditions.org.

The author is grateful to the print and online editors in whose publications the reprinted poems in this volume originally appeared, sometimes in different versions with different titles.

The selected poems were first published in *Alaska Quarterly Review*, *American Poetry Review*, *Ariel*, *Arts & Letters*, *Beloit Poetry Journal*, *Cortland Review*, *Crab Orchard Review*, *Croton Review*, *Dunes Review*, *Georgia Review*, *Image*, *Indiana Review*, *Iowa Review*, *Kestrel*, *Kenning*, *Kenyon Review*, *Michigan Quarterly Review*, *Mid-American Review*, *Miramar*, *New Virginia Review*, *Ocho*, *Paterson Review*, *Poet Lore*, *Poetry*, *Poetry Northwest*, *Prairie Schooner*, *Shenandoah*, *Southern Humanities Review*, *Southern Poetry Review*, *Southern Review*, *Tar River Review*, *West Branch*, and *Yarrow*.

"Einstein on Mercer Street" was first performed as a piece for orchestra and voice by the New Music Ensemble, Pittsburgh, Pennsylvania, 2002. Composer: Kevin Puts. It is available on the CD titled *Against the Emptiness* from New Dynamic Records.

"If I Were a Swan" was set to music by Kevin Puts and premiered by the Austin, Texas–based chorus Conspirare, under the direction of Craig Hella Johnson, on September 27, 2012. It is available on CD, performed by the Baltimore Symphony Orchestra.

I would also like to acknowledge *The Devil's Child*, the one book not included in this collection. Its continuous narrative and the tone of the book made it impossible to fit among these other poems. Nonetheless, I would like to thank Kathryn Harris and the real Barbara for making that difficult book possible.

Thanks also to the editors of the following journals in which the new poems were first published: "5 Moons," "Edward Hopper's *Automat*," "Unfurl," *Southern Poetry Review*; "Elegance," "Mute Swan," *New Ohio Review*; "The Muskrat," *Antioch Review*; "Lesson," *Bellevue Review*; "Reading the *Smithsonian* Magazine," *Michigan Quarterly Review*; "The Bar Mitzvah," "Every Day I Touch Things," "Tiny Fish," *Image*; "Poem for Record Players," *Crab Orchard Review*; "The Sex Life of Anacondas," "Snoring," *Georgia Review*; "Bees," *If Bees Are Few: A Hive of Bee Poems*, University of Minnesota Press; "July 20, 1944," *Miramar*; "On a Day That Bombs," "Protection," *New England Review*; "Refrigerator," *New*

Letters; "Asian Carp," *Pleiades*; "Taxol," *Numero Cinq*; "Cancer Support Group with Painting by Monet," "Speed," *Prairie Schooner*; "The War," *Cortland Review*; "Getting Free," "View from Space," "Pike," *Southern Review*.

My deep gratitude to Ted Kooser, who appreciated my work enough to invite me to put this volume together. To my faithful pal Sydney Lea, who's been reading my poems for decades now. To my Traverse City poet friends, especially Teresa Scollon, Anne Marie Oomen, Jennifer Steinorth, and Catherine Turnbull. To my geographically scattered writer friends, especially those at Rainier Writing Workshop. To my family. And to my beloved husband: first reader and first friend, to whom this book is dedicated.

INTRODUCTION | Ted Kooser

In the opening paragraphs of *Walden*, Henry David Thoreau writes, "I, on my side, require of every writer, first or last, a simple and sincere account of his own life, and not merely what he has heard of other men's lives; some such account as he would send to his kindred from a distant land; for if he has lived sincerely, it must have been in a distant land to me."

There's an important suggestion behind those words: The author whom Thoreau seeks and admires makes an offer of his words *to someone else*. We might think that a transaction too obvious to point to, but there is a great deal of poetry written and published today that turns its back (sometimes with apparent disdain) upon the reader. During the past one hundred years of the Modern and now Postmodern ages, a great deal of our poetry has turned away from communication. At a poetry festival a few years ago, I heard a noted American poet say that it is the responsibility of readers to educate themselves to a level that they can understand what poets write. Thoreau would no doubt have scoffed at such arrogance.

One of my purposes in editing this series is to present the work of American poets who are doing their best to make gifts to their readers— to communicate, to charm, to persuade. Jared Carter's *Darkened Rooms of Summer* and Connie Wanek's *Rival Gardens* are just such gifts, as is this third book.

Fleda Brown's book is indeed the sincere account of a life, though it is, to use Thoreau's word, "simple" only in that it is open-handed and conversational. These are not simple poems by any means, but neither are they intentionally difficult. They don't hide anything, nor are they coy, nor are they clever for the sake of cleverness, but they are indeed a life, offered to us with candor, care, and generosity, a life like yours and mine, in which challenges are faced and learned from. Brown's successive poems, in book after book, offer us a record of a poet's development first as a person and second as an accomplished literary artist.

The first poem here, "Fishing with Blood," from Brown's first book, shows us the poet as a child, curious and observant, attentive to her parents and the immediate surroundings, and "Mushrooms," the last poem of the new poems, shows us the same attentiveness, but now the poet has grown older, and the protections of her early life have fallen back and away. You hold the first of these poems in your left hand and the last in your right, and in between is the carefully and beautifully presented record of the life of a talented and influential American poet. And a person who reaches, in welcome, to you.

THE WOODS ARE ON FIRE

Backfires

The woods are on fire.
The woods are seething and blistering.
Matisse, stuck in his wheelchair, is scissoring shapes,
directing his assistant to pin them to a board.
Beethoven is solving musical problems inside the soundless
chamber of his head. Elizabeth Bishop is sitting in the waiting room
studying naked women with her poised intellect. She cries out.
Oh no. It's not her, but from the other room.
The wildfire of her heart is about to cross the gap cut by the firemen.
A small backfire has been set near the bigger one to use up
the oxygen that fuels it. You have to know where
the bigger one is headed. You do not know where
the bigger one is headed, so it is always the backfires.
Even the water in the hoses can catch fire.
The fire is not really in the water, but the water gets drunk up.
If you were on fire I would roll you in a blanket as I have been told.
There is a cardinal out there against the snow! Such a cliché,
but a dramatic example of the tiny backfire that keeps us
from burning alive.

I

FROM *FISHING WITH BLOOD* | 1988

Garden

My father is up at 6:30
in his bare chest and pajama bottoms,
whistling among the tomatoes,
brooding over the ruffled petunias
along the driveway wall. I watch him
through the screen door
where the morning has not yet
touched me, thin as a nightgown.
He looks like a circus man, performing
tricks too small for his muscles,
cross-pollinating petunias
with a tiny paintbrush, lifting
away their yellow powder.
Also he looks like a huge eye
down on the tiny mechanics
of the world. I watch his deliberate
move, his mingling of dust.
My mother is still in bed, soft as clay,
anonymous as sheets. She would get up
and start in on last night's dishes,
if she had the energy.
It seems we have drawn it out
of her, that the sun is wrong to shine.
Her energy is out there, loose
barefoot in the garden, pajama strings
loose, careless of himself, careful
of the type: the Big Boy tomatoes,
the Hungarian yellow peppers.
He might be no one, in the flesh,
except for his green orchestration,
his rows. He whistles "Ode to Joy,"
getting it right, yes, this is it,
is it, ties each note on its trellis

like a good child climbing
to heaven. I stick out my tongue
against the bitter screen, to taste
whether I am a woman or a man, and
whose I am, and for what I was made.

To Mark, My Retarded Brother, Who Lived 20 Years and Learned to Speak 300 Words

Nobody has any business but me, to tell how
you came home, a white ball up pitted concrete steps,
home to our grandmother's swirled carpet.
Knitted bundle, you wailed clues of that soft
rotten, that misconnection, that sever, that spasm
that broke your mother's heart into blank starts.
You drug your feet, child.

Across the wood floor your twirling walker,
the rattling dance lurched down
fourteen steps: you were never lucky.
Your spilled blood flowed like menses, expected
rupture, bombardment of corners, ridges, juts.
The record player sat on the chest by the window:
blood, spit, and dirt where you plied
that delicate spinning with your scratched hands.
"Getting to know you," know you, you and
Deborah Kerr on the vowels, one long happy drool.
Hollyhock ladies on the sill, I lined up for you.
With a towel, I held that white head
that smashed into the blank floor
and everything, I think, I could ever know.
You grew to be a crane, your head
bobbling on the tops of your friends
who took you to play with perfect aplomb.
Little citizens already, in the grass,
they calculated games you could not wreck.
I was the one who ran barefoot, terror light,
to grab you loping onto Garland Street,
laughing. I could have bashed in your head,
unsubtle brother, smiling outline.

Angel face, pushing to break with rudiments,
the best word for you is *unused*.

So your ankles drew up solemnly,
wrists in. The spasm locked. When I came to you
in your sterile steel circus, the last clowns
had gone home. Malicious beard raked your face.
On your head, practical blond hair razed
at short attention.
You seemed so heavy you would never float away.
Then you sank into your coffin in flannel pajamas,
the warmest bed you ever felt.

Arch

Every day she walked to school through
the wet grass and along the confusion
of steel, rising to be the new field house.
Every day she walked home, stopping to watch
the huge arches flash with welders
and men yell instructions across the beams.

"It was an ordinary Wednesday afternoon,"
she would say after that, although
it became ordinary only when something happened
to measure it by.

She had crossed the field to Terry Village
where her mother was hanging diapers
on the line and her brother was throwing toys
off his blue quilt. She was standing
on the porch eating a Fig Newton
when she happened to look up and see
the great arch lean and the tiny body drop,
in slow motion, like all catastrophe.

She remembered the little arms waving,
the tremor when the steel struck,
and the dust rising like smoke.
She imagined the body, final
as a bag of sand. She thought of the workman
that morning, buttoning a khaki shirt,
leaving for work, lighting a Lucky Strike
on his way out the door, telling someone good-bye.
She thought of the omens in a regular day,
the arch she walked under ten minutes ago.
She felt like an angel, transcending events.
She thought which muscles she might have tried
if she had been the workman, suddenly needing to fly.

For Grandmother Beth

Just one scandalous year past
our grandmother's death, the second wife
stood homely and trembling ankle-deep
in the lake, taking on water and family
at once. Once, she told me, your grandfather
found the box of hair your grandmother
saved when she had it bobbed. She said
he cried, and I tried to imagine both
wives working it out in heaven. He took
this second one, taught her theories
of economics, gave her his grown children
and grandchildren, money, and houses.
They used to sit at the kitchen table and eat
prunes, the same table where he ate
prunes with my grandmother. Regularity
took him to ninety-five, although
the last year in the nursing home he
couldn't remember who she was, and even
years before that, at the lake, he'd
call her by his dead wife's name. No,
Harry, she'd say, it's Beth, Beth, and
lead him back to where he meant to
go. She never touched the money he left
her, saved it for his children, took
in roomers and lived on interest. Now
she's dead, and all Garth Avenue is
gone from me, from us, the house,
the lilies of the valley on the north
side, oh, it would be a long list, and
who cares now but us. This is what I

have to say for her, who held a place
and saved everything as if she had no
needs, or wishes, except to be no
trouble at all, and to die quickly, a
light turned out to save electric bills.

A Plain Philosophical Choice

Blake Jett in his stripped-down Ford
could roar off with the loose girls. We
walked, cradling Western civilization
in hardback against our breasts.
We were the smart track, and we knew it.
In gym class and homeroom, they
mixed everything up like democracy,
but we knew their signs.
We gave them blue ink, wide
margins, engravable words.

Yet one by one, we came into our hormones,
plebeian as Kotex. Under our skirts,
the bulge of equipment, buried like sin.
Voluminous notes were exchanged on the matter.
Nina Spalding's tight skirts risked
as much as our parents warned, and
overnight, she was gone, with her stomach.
Ricky and Elvis conflicted down our bulletin boards,
a plain philosophical choice: country-club white
or the deep rumble from the edge of black.

A person could settle for anything.
The school could blow up, the town, the USA.
A person could go crazy with waiting.
After school, a person could take a certain bus,
to sit with a certain boy, and leave
her arrogant friends to walk.
Down the hillside,
the ribbon of buses was always numbered.
Inside, their handrails worn to steel,

the wounds of their gray seats picked bare.
Soon the drivers would grind their motors
one after the other
and roll their yellow machines downhill
until they broke away like pollen.

Out Back

Once I heard an owl
through a tunnel from the moon,
imagined it huge
in its eyes, floating down
from the woods toward the lake.

All things moved down,
the life of trees clawed
at the hill, roots rolled
downhill in rivulets
beneath the lantern.
Behind my back, the cottage
slid toward the water
like an ice cube melting.

"See the eyes of the owl,"
my grandmother said, holding
the lantern to the trees
where something stirred, but
even the eyes had closed
into the awful dark.

My grandmother stood lean
and erect, her hair already loose
for the night and waved down
her back like the real woman
in a fairy tale. She said
my name, which was also her
name, said it out at the night
to make me appear, and hold.

Canoe

This is how Alan rebuilt
the Thompson Brothers canoe:
He loosened the gunnels,
pulled the tacks
out, unscrewed the keel,
and the old canvas fell away.
He fixed a couple of broken
ribs, set the frame inside
a canvas hammock
pulled with block and tackle.
Inside that, he set
concrete blocks for weight,
and wiggled the frame
for a week until the canvas
loved its shape. He wrapped
and tacked the ends, coated
the canvas with sealer
hard enough to sand.
Then he screwed the gunnels
on, then the brass
at bow and stern, then
to keel. This is how much
love there is in the fingers,
in the shapes given to the eye
when the eye hardly knows
what it sees. The fingers
draw back the shape
of sliding through
the water, of evening
and morning, of coming
along the cusp
of light and dark
with no sound, moving

as if moving were a wish
pulling itself.
The paddle goes down
like muscle, a faint slap.
The shape is the channel,
the ribbed basket,
the lightness of breaking
through, the suspension
between sky and floor,
a sigh, a stretch
of canvas like a drawn
bow, lean as fingers.

Whaler

I teach my niece Elizabeth
to let down her oars,
then pull and lift with mine.
Our wake smooths
like a tail. Elizabeth says
we are a dragonfly,
double-oared. I think
we are an old woman,
our low whaler spreading
the reeds with wide hips,
sloshing hollow.
Elizabeth talks nonsense
about Indians from Moscow
who spray their hair
with Raid. She imagines
molecules, red against
green, jostling the lake
like Jell-O. Sure.
And there were wildcats once
across the road, eating
the Knowles's chickens
and eating the loser of
hide-and-seek, who
would be thrown to
the night by the boys.
Flashlight/night,
lofting and sinking, we make
these exultations of oars.
We're always close to flying.
We always plan to fly.

Catching Turtles

The slightest drip of a paddle
is too much. Let the canoe slide
by itself into the rushes and lily pads.
Lean far over the bow, your arm
a dead stick, drifting its shadow
through the water.
                You scoop
a turtle from behind, snatch it
from the log, a hard bulge
escaped inward.
                Snapper, you grab between
your careful fingers, arched
across the shell, back from
their craning dinosaur necks,
their mute bird beaks.
                When you miss, you hear
the soft blip. Bubbles trail off
in deep, iridescent angles.
You don't catch them
for any reason. They scratch around
the canoe's wet bottom, leaving
stinking pools, and you bring them
two miles home. For days they wallow
and scrape their brown helmets
in the aluminum tub by the dock.
You add mussel shells and a Petoskey
stone for company. You feed them
worms, grubs, and a granddaddy longlegs.
You get used to hearing them.
When you go to swim, or sit
at the end of the dock feeding
the clamoring swans at sunset,
you start believing that skidding

and shucking against the tub
             is their real voice.
But when you let them go,
they ease down the rocks and slide
unruffled and heavy as fishing lead
under the alien weeds
in righteous silence.

Fishing with Blood

They have waited for us in the country,
keeping the catfish fed,
bushhogging the pond banks clear.

We must pull up a chair on the long porch
while they hold down Sunday afternoon,
circling their voices on episodes.

Then we can take the cane poles
from against the chimney
to find what is left of luck.

Small bream toy with the ball of blood
on the hook, so when the big cat
strikes, it is more than I am

ready for, driving my line down.
The great ache of the pole quivers
toward heaven, before the line snaps.

For hours we watch the cork bob
and dive, raising clues.
We wade to our necks for it.

We cast a flounder rig, its hooks
vicious in the pond. It claws the cork,
thrashes fourteen pounds of catfish

against the bank. The line snaps again.
We take the gift of our fish tale
in the pink evening up to the porch.

They draw it to them like a prodigal son,
full of flaws, but redeemable.
They go to work on it.

Apalachee Bay

The oystermen of Apalachee Bay stand
in their small boats. They spread their tongs
down from the boats, biting down bubbles.

The oystermen do blind men's work, rocked
in the visible cup of land. From the shallow
deep they dredge the green-black rocks,
scatter them over the trays, throw out
the halves and sand-filled wastes.
The oystermen cheerfully curse and rake
again under their shaken reflections.
In the keeper bins, the knotted clusters
clamp their wet mouths shut.

Up the docks, five women stand all day
at their five stalls under the windows,
shouting over the whistling saws that grind
open the oysters of Apalachee Bay.
The women's surgical fingers flick brine
and gather muscle. Through the glass,
the women watch their men in the boats
come nosing in, shuffling the water's sky.

Below the legs of the women, five chutes
open to the bay, heaping shells back,
greenish, bleached, translucent, out
of their sight. The men rumbling up
from the docks with their wheelbarrows
eye the size of the heaps for a sure thing
against the vague roll of the sea.

At the windows, the women's eyes are sharp
for quality, measuring gift and giver, the slits
of their eyes more telling than their mouths.

The Scholar's Cat

I've never seen anyone take to a cat
the way you have. Three stillborn litters
she's had, and you keep hoping she'll give over

one fuzzy live one, one mewing paddypaw.
For such a growler, you are easy to this
fragile cat, who sits in the street,

mindless, who goes out and struts back
two days later, black tail puffed
from some night vision, or some Tom.

She shadows under the sofa, tail twitching,
scratches on the bedroom door at eight,
begs expensive food, whines and slithers

in constant heat. You stumble through
your days, insomniac, shoving at your own
bounds, and there she is, curled

and purring. Her spring fur flies
away like dandelion shafts. Your spring
hair grows long, curls out from your ears.

You don't shave for days. Huge raccoon circles
spread under your eyes. You read
yourself vague. But at three, when you've

long ago kissed me and every wriggling,
talking thing asleep, out of the night sky,
Zang! That cat hits the screen like a bat,

splayed, claws into every nerve. You lumber
to the door and let her in respectfully.
She curls in your lamplight. She is, for you,

the simple purr of nature's simple engine.
She sleeps when her eyes shut, she eats
when her stomach fusses, she makes love

when some blind itch shoves her, startled,
out the door. If her skinny self
concocted reproductions, the whole

sweet song would circle back around
and leave you pleased as punch
that nature knows so blooming much.

Saving a Life

You keep your illness, examining
its vague and shifty facets
like a jeweler as we take our daily walk.
By Thanksgiving, clouds and drizzle set in
and someone wants to die
on the railroad tracks.
Innocently, we circle the station
into revolving lights that wheel up
one after the other, official vehicles,
raising a static of news.
The police are not going to let anybody die.
They are fingers of a hand across
all tracks, their voices surgically calm
in the night. The man is either drunk or drunk
with misery, throwing his reasons against them:
his grandfather dead, his little cousin
dead, his wife fucking some other man,
hey man, he yells down the dark,
there's nobody left.
Reasons enough, the cops should say,
nodding their heads. What the train can do
to him is hardly anything, we think.
Go ahead, we don't blame you, we want
to yell. We think he might take his grief
in his arms like a rock, then,
and roll away just in time, weak-kneed,
but owning the trouble himself.
Safer, they talk him to submission,
his wife arriving barefoot in the cold.
They lead him to the cars like a prisoner,
dividing his suffering among them
until each piece seems like nothing,
until he is too poor to argue.

He Says How It Was

1

Jaycee Park is where Wayman Fuller hid
in the bushes to waylay the colored who ducked
through at night on their way home
to the Quarters. (That was 1958 in Jackson,
Mississippi, language like a coin worn
faceless.) Across Bailie Avenue
is Virgil Street. It humps up, held then
at the top by four white houses, square
as books, with attached garages, hung
with wrenches, screwdrivers, pliers
on pegs. But from there the lean
began to roll and pitch, down
to the far end of Virgil Street. Beyond that
was only City Creek, the wide sewer
where the Baptist Church quit.

2

Five houses up on our side lived Lucky Cade,
pale as ashes. I loved him like a brother,
but he sold his bones to queers,
slow cruising, quiet, from Bailie Avenue.
His mother had black shoe polish hair
and an old man. And this is true:
They spooned poison in the oatmeal,
fed it to his grandbabies. She got off,
but he was electrocuted.
Daddy went to watch. You could do that
then. I remember he came home,
set his teeth on the edge of the sink,
and threw up. Mrs. Cade's next man Snooky
stacked boxes at Liberty Grocery Mart.

Snooky had a hand wrapped
with a white towel, soaked with sweat
and ringed in salt. They went dancing
Saturday nights, in spite of that hand.

3

The house next to the creek
belonged to Mr. Thigpen, before he died.
That's where the oak tree was,
with the wisteria, a mother of a tree,
dark, dripping with vines,
lacing black over the dirt yard.
In the spring, purple swelled
like a bruise, awesome. In back,
Mr. Thigpen had thirty-five fig trees
which he paid me to pick. Early,
just before the sun, my gloved hands
held the finest bulbs, just ripe
and sharp, from the birds
that sailed and pecked at first light.
I hired me six colored at half-price
plus a sack of figs we set outside
the fence, and I kept the difference.
Everybody was happy, except
Mr. Thigpen, when he saw those
chocolate boys in his trees
among the fruit, rescuing it
from blacker fate.

4

When he died, the Sullivans moved in.
(That wisteria crashed blooms
against the porch, spring
after spring.) Saturdays, his momma
made me and Robert Earl Sullivan

shell peas in the front room. One day
his daddy barged in, glued the hungry
shine of his drunk eyes
on Robert Earl, and raked his paw
down a cheek. Robert Earl pumped
a fist into his teeth. The cracks
between filled with red.
My breath dropped below the shells
of peas. The sofa leg shoved
through the floor, the shotgun
went off through the roof.
When the cops came, Mr. Sullivan
asked them in for ice tea.
Corn bread, peas, and tea,
that's all they ever ate.

5

Grandma Sullivan had a boyfriend.
When he went away, there was a string
of them after that. It was glorious
when she came to stay. She would get drunk
and play the piano, and sing hymns.
Robert Earl and Tommy Dale and me,
fixed for a dance in our polished white shoes
and white shirts, had to stand
lined up for her to admire
at the piano. Fine young bucks,
she would say. When we came home
at three, she would still
be singing, "I Couldn't Hear Nobody Pray."
By then, the five-year-old was drunk,
too, on beer tea.

6

All of us had gardens. In the spring,
the only mule left in town brought heaps of manure
from somewhere, and the smell was rich
and thick, of things packed down, cooking
the soil, pulling onions, tomatoes,
squash, corn, and beans out of the dark.

Emily Dickinson's Love

This is why you hear the spasm in my verse:
I am in danger. The butcher's boy brings in

the red slabs. He pedals through yawning streets
where shops rise yeasty along the banks.

Here, even the stair's toothed grin curls
toward my room. Downstairs, eddies of guests.

Against the turbulence, I put the vice to my words.
And lately, a new calm—someone I love!

For someone, I fold my hair and sit in patient
white, immaculately worded, expecting the bare sun

unveiled. It is dark. Outside my window,
frogs harrumph for love, and crickets blither.

You cannot imagine my love's abyss of possible
names. I am pruning, finding the one,

although I know the stairs stand guard between us.
My love is a stake on the polished floor below.

Softly, I close my door, straining to hear his whistle,
his cordial refrain, to press it to my sheet

like a rose, its dizzy whorl stain
against the white. You know the spasm

in my verse? The dash against the word?
The closet room, furnished with codes?

Love, for Instance

Love, for instance, is a setup.
Like in Chagall's painting, *The Birthday*,
you would think every object in the room broke loose
by spontaneous combustion. But love has been planned
to happen that way for some time, although
this occasion is new. When her lover was thinking
flowers, you must know he figured hormones
and could already imagine the wings of her collar,
her breasts like wings, Mary Poppins, transported,
unmoored. And look at her eyes as she kisses him,
wide open, deliberate as his flowers. She watches him
roll out of her mouth like a ghostly language
and drift down her back, *en train*.
She has made him up.
You know she has made him up because he has no arms
and can't even be a real lover, rubber-necked and armless.
He couldn't even hold down a job.
How wonderful it is to get things into that condition,
to make even the paisley print on the wall wiggle
like tadpoles! It is especially a good idea
since outside one window, a row of guardhouses
plods whitely down the street, and outside the other,
nothing but a ladder of more windows.
With love, you can have a red floor, and rise above it.
But don't expect to be believed, entirely:
the melon, the cake, and the stool are round-eyed,
but it is feigned innocence, not surprise.
The blunt knife is aimed at the hole in the cake,
a little joke. The bulging purse lies on the edge
of the table where it might fall to somebody's ruin.
The clincher is the stool, absolutely round
and black, bouncing off its legs, a hole
you fall into just under the flowers.

from "O'Keeffe"

She Learns to Walk

Years later, Georgia claimed
she remembered exactly
the quilt she lay on
in Sun Prairie, Wisconsin,
before she could walk, its
red stars and white flowers,
her Aunt Winnie's flowered
dress and golden hair.
Light rose to her fingers
from the half-dreams
of childhood, and sank,
the way dreams do
on waking. An ache, a vague
joy is left, and Rorschach
shapes riding the cusp
of what one takes to be
real, the material world or
the dream, depending
on one's education.

The assignment was to sketch
from a plaster cast of a baby's
hand. The sister
at the convent school wanted
it larger, like a sign,
and light as an angel lifting
up to God. Even then,
Georgia understood in
her black heart the
subversion required for art.
She made everything
bigger than it should be
and temporarily delicate.

She put influences away, began
her life again on hands
and knees with charcoal and rough
paper, rubbing shapes until
her body ached, a lunatic, working
into her own, unknown. By June
she needed blue: for two
thin flames, one a cocked
elbow, Georgia exact, a flute's
height and edge, hungry as jazz,
little stomachs of blue pulled
into the rise. She lived, then,
entirely in her body, her blue
blood breathing no air but
rising like mercury out of her will.

"At last, a woman
on paper!" Stieglitz said in
New York when he hung her
raw intentions where
Rodin, Picasso, Cézanne, had been.
"But Stieglitz," a critic said,
"all these pictures say is 'I want
to have a baby.'"
"That's fine," Stieglitz replied.
"A woman has painted a picture
that says she wants to have a baby."

In Palo Duro Canyon, Georgia saw
long lines of cows, made them blood-
red eggs, raising yellow dust between
two mountains' bones:
her nightmare of falling in.
Then she painted the evening star

six times. Its vacant center
broadcast yellow, orange, red, what
happens when you look too long, until
one star gives the sky
its meaning. The star is not
what you see but the rash result
of it. The star slips back from
your memory and is lost or free.

A New Yorker Visits Her Exhibition

A man in a brown vest
observes jack-in-the-pulpits, painted
over and over, closer and
closer to the swelled
spike, the slit
of light. The trumpet flower
pillowed white toward its yawning
shaft. The sunflower spread
like a whore for the
bees. Georgia sits bolt upright
in the corner, enduring his
plod and gawk. Her hands lock
their secrets around
each other. She turns
her flowers loose. If this
man had been the one who stuck their seeds
into the soil, they would go on
without him, or die
of weeds, no matter, growing
again in wilder transformations. He
stands before Georgia's monstrous
calla lilies, hands
in his pockets. Perhaps he has almost
discovered his small
importance in this process, and has

begun to look into his heart for
another point of view. She
watches the symmetry
of his limbs as they turn and
return almost against their will to
the same vaginal tease: a star, a bell-
shaped cry, "Come in, come in!"

She Marries the Photographer

STIEGLITZ

I focus on her thigh, the wings
of her eyebrows. She is so lean
the film can't find her, but
finds her messages, which
she has made to look like
herself. Posing makes her itch.

O'KEEFFE

Stieglitz talks all the time,
drawing the line of his thoughts
around his friends. Lord!
I want my gallery white
and curtainless, the colors
exactly where they should be.

O'KEEFFE

When we sweep the relatives out,
Lake George blackens and steams
toward winter; I can paint nude
in my shanty. Stieglitz walks down
for mail from New York, his black
cape flapping like a crow for news.

STIEGLITZ

So now she needs the West.
Its bald light dissolves me

from her consciousness. All is new.
She paints bones six months a year.
In late fall, she comes to me
from the badlands, brazen with canvases.

The telegraph boy flags me down
in Abiquiu. By the time
I fly East, there is nothing to do
but rip the pink satin lining
from his coffin and sit all night
sewing plain white linen in.

An Expert Explains Her Work

Anything pared to the bone
needs interpretation, so
no one will be bored. You can't
say look there, and there. Only
here, like a devotional.
Once, Georgia O'Keeffe stole
an immaculate black river stone
from a friend's table with no
explanation, and she
is well-known to have painted
that same shape in a number of
excuses: the single alligator pear,
the sunflower's eye,
the obdurate moon,
the hole in the pelvis bone. How
far it is to eternity, and how
little we have to go on! Stripped
of flesh, the pelvis bone
is capable of flying
open like a camera lens.

Then she was forever
painting, like a curse, versions
of the door in the patio wall
at Abiquiu. It took her ten
years to buy that house, that
door, which had once been
sold for two cows, a bushel of
corn, and a serape. Still, it made
no apologies, a rectangular
door in a patio wall,
sharpened and scrupulous,
a place on the wall to
let your eyes
stop and collect their forces.
If anything went in or out, you
could see, and put a stop
to it, or be the only one
waiting, thus, the most beautiful.

II

FROM *DO NOT PEEL THE BIRCHES* | 1993

Elvis at the End of History

It was him, Elvis, sheepishly
stepping out of the outhouse,
looking better than ever, the way
some old men slim down and loosen
their lines. He had left the door open,
the lid slightly ajar on the women's
hole. As usual, I forgave him
everything. I acted normal, as if
I hadn't been waiting under the trees,
last night's full chamber pot
balanced in my hand. I could have
said at any point in my life
that he was the one I was waiting for,
looking sleepily down from the stage,
seeing but not seeing me,
granting me reprieve in an instant
from my life, but holding me in it
like a star. It's like if you ask
for Jesus, Jesus comes. It's never
the way you think. There he was,
hair flopped over his eyes,
coming out of the last outhouse left
along the lake, and it there
only because of the grandfather clause.
This was the end of our history
together, all that strangeness
in the crotch, the pulse hammering
the bass line, real life and art
straining to fuse, to end all
history. I was hearing in my mind
Won't you wear my ring,
around your neck? but it sounded
like the sweet core of good taste,

like the gospel fleshed out,
saddened down to honky-tonk.
"Excuse me," he said. "The older I get,
the more often I have to pee."
I agreed. I might have been humming
to myself, sometimes I don't know
when I'm doing it. I can be
treble and bass at the same time.

Do Not Peel the Birches

In his time,
germs were found to be everywhere,
especially in his ball-and-socket joint
which was welded together by tuberculosis germs
before pasteurized milk became a rule.
Grandfather ordered his shirts done at home
because (he demonstrated) the downtown launderer
spat germs on the iron to test the heat.
Flies (he caught midflight in his cupped hand)
could crop-dust germs over lunch,
and one's mouth grew germs quickly enough
between the meal and the toothbrush.

He gathered us at Central Lake every summer
to learn the rules. He explained the use of
lie (to recline) and *lay* (to place or put):
because of his lame leg, he could *lie*
comfortably only in the canoe, so we must
lay it gently on the sand, keeping its
irreplaceable wooden frame from rocks.

At Central Lake, one could get hold
of things that go wrong. One could nail a sign
on the birches to save their delicate skins.
One could avoid shampoos or detergents that foam
the lake. One could rinse diapers in a bucket
far up the hill to filter the dirty water
through the ground. One could wait
one full hour after meals, and only swim
across the lake guarded by the rowboat.
One could follow the rules and get results.
When Grandfather was ninety-four
he was still getting results.

In the cottage, he heard the wind chimes
answer to an ancient wind.
Someone pulled diapason
on the pump organ, and he called back
a perfectly metered hymn.
Muttering through the fir trees, he
was able at last to discuss the day's mail
with his dead wife, who knew what to do.
And every morning and evening,
he stoppered his ears, hitched his lame leg
over the dock, and buried himself in the lake,
only his nose rising for air. He broke through
the elements as cleanly as a machine.

A Long and Happy Life

Today particularly, my father seals up
his camera in a Tupperware bowl
with silica gel to keep it dry.
He wraps large rubber bands cut
from an old inner tube around the bowl.
Aunt Cleone is fixing a bowl of raw oatmeal,
yogurt, and sesame seeds.
She takes a damp undershirt from the refrigerator
and unwraps enough purslane and mint leaves
to grind on her cereal. They are arguing
about sex. My father says women don't like it.
Cleone tells how she and Uncle Bob
made love every day after swimming, how she
wore him out. My mother takes her toast
to the deck and watches a huge jay land
spread-legged on the rail,
scattering goldfinches away from the feeder.
This is as close to the facts
as I can get. It is a Thursday, 9:20,
after a cold swim. Cleone enters her twenty-third
year without a cold or any other sickness.
My mother has almost succeeded at solitude.
Even the jay is no sorrow to her.

Learning to Dance

When we waltzed with the senior citizens
at the Pappy Burnett Pavilion,
I felt how you moved slick as a cowboy,
my own rough bones clicking beside
you, trying to move the way trying can't
go. I loved you, turning in yourself
like a loose skin, and the woman
who danced with her broom, and the old man
round-dancing, his shirt open over
his heavy belly, an old, old grace
feeding him from the bass
of the country band. I've always
wanted to dance. Aspen leaves tambourine
in the wind, needles flare from the tamarack
branch like ballet skirts, and that
Wednesday of the Central Lake Pavilion Dance
travels miles in place, turning
and returning to its original dark.
Afterward, I pulled off my swimsuit in the lake
and held you next to me, learning
from your heart and the slap-slap of waves
on stones. What is it wants us to know
where to step? Each pause
brings us tight against the mouth
of the earth, and then we raise one
foot like the flame of a candle.
Our bodies move in and out of the space
we've held to be true, and something else
sees each half turn as the whole dance.

After the Rain

While we are having breakfast
on the screened-in porch, waffles
with blueberries, my mother wrinkles
into tears over nothing, some
remembrance. She is always
giving in. The outside world is
wrung out, too, exhausted
with last night's rain, darkened
and earthly. On the black tree trunk,
a nuthatch pitches itself
upside down and sideways,
pecking wildly for bugs
under the bark. A chickadee
is a quick breath, lifting
off a limb. I want
to take my mother's hands,
but they are almost transparent,
terrible on the table.
Her body hunkers like a vase,
accumulating sorrows. It is
a Chinese vase, slender
at the neck, glazed
on the inside. In my mouth
are scrambled eggs
I have to eat or never get up
again. I sit through adolescence,
adulthood, safely
into menopause. The eggs soften
in my mouth, harden on
my plate, yellow ruffles.
Blue flowered oilcloth clings
to the table. My mother's hands
keep on fluttering

outward. No use, no use.
I pass her a waffle, butter,
a jug of pure
maple syrup, too heavy to pour.
I line up these items
in front of her. Hope
tries to get out of my chest.
It sounds like my heart, but it's
furious, hungry, light as a bird.

Loon Cries

Unless there is a loon cry in a book, the poetry has gone out of it.
CARL SANDBURG

Three loons appear in this poem, two
on one side of the canoe, one
on the other, but

not stable. One drops down
to nothing, emerges two minutes later
twenty feet away, quavering

his black beak's cold cries
across us to the others like a natural
bridge: oo-AH-hoo. Three loon cries

arise in this poem
from a hollow carved out
of itself, the slosh of what it says

to itself, not to us.
We four in the canoe sit
in the open AH, riding low as loons.

No one knows who feels
what, or how much. The grieving
syllables lie over us, untouchable

oo-AH-hoo, yodeled
oo-AH-hoo. Oh Lord, if we knew
what we can take from each other, and what

we have to leave alone,
if we knew which maniacal dives
the universe was thinking of all along.

Night Swimming

We are without our men, hers dead
ten years, mine far away, the water
glassy warm. My old aunt already stands
half in. All I see is the white half,
her small old breasts like bells,
almost nice as a girl's. Then we hardly
feel the water, a drag on the nipples,
a brush on the crotch, like making love
blind, only the knives of light
from the opposite shore, the shudders
of our swimming breaking it up.
We let the water get next to us
and into the quick of losses we don't
have to talk about. We swim out
to where the dock goes blank,
and we are stranded, abandoned good flesh
in a black of glimmering. We each fit
our skin exactly. After a while
we come out of the water slick as eels,
still swimming, straight-backed,
breasts out, up to the porch,
illuminate, sexy as hell, inspired.

My Father Takes My Retarded Brother Sailing

They tack up and down
all morning. Mark trailing one hand

in the waves, crying his hard
gull-cries of joy, my father pointing out

bright flags on shore, which are
us, waving

them on, until
the sudden commotion of sail, jabber

of cleats, swingabout of
boat, pivot of Central Lake on

my father's foot, caught at that moment
in a rope,

my father hanging neither up
nor down, thrashing under, using,
              maybe using up his lungs
to catch that child who hardly knows
water from air. The thought,

oh yes, the thought settles
in my heart: part of me

goes down, drowned, the perfect part
splashes back
to shore. And then years
later, here I come,

bringing out the towels, willing
as a murderer, reformed, but sentenced

anyway, to this life, to this
abundant life in which they have both

come back, my father's ankle bloody
from the rope, my purple-lipped

brother riding his shoulders,
            uncontrollably babbling.

If I Were a Swan

I would ride high
above my own white
weight. I would ride
through the lightening
of the earth
and the darkening,
stillness and turbulence
coming on in the core
of me, and spreading
to the hard rain,
to the dazzle. Leaves
would turn, but I
would keep my eyes
in my head, watching
for grasses. This
is what I would know
deeply: the feathering
of my bones
against the bank.
For the rest,
I would be the easiest
wave, loving just enough
for nature's sake.
The world would move
under me and I would
always be exactly
where I am, dragonflies
angling around my head.
Under the black mask
of my face, I would think
swan, swan,
which would be nothing

but a riding, a hunger,
a ruffle more pointed
than wind and waves,
and a hot-orange
beak like an arrow.

Dock

Say *dock, dock*: it's just a hollow
of itself, the way the foot
echoes between wood and water,
the plank, plank of it
like piano keys, growing hollower
farther out under the stars.
Listen to the way *dock*'s closed in
by the tongue on one side, pushed out
at the far end toward the lake
with a duck-sound, quack-
sound, where they congregate
for crumbs. It's even a tongue,
itself, saying nothing but
what you bump against it.
Or an arm, reaching out. Here
you're willing to make yourself sociable,
declare yourself separate
from the trees. "Dock here,"
you offer. Here is a place
to stop. And it's true. Indeed,
I have to stop at the end,
and think. The reason
for walking out here is
how the end goes blunt.
You feel your blood turn back
toward the heart, but
for an instant, you imagine,
it longs to keep moving out,
like Roadrunner at the edge of a cliff,
keeping on with nothing built
to hold him up. Turning back,
I carve a cul-de-sac in the air,
which is a comfort, and a sadness.

A Few Lines from Rehoboth Beach

Dear friend you were right: the smell of fish and foam
and algae makes one green smell together. It clears
my head. It empties me enough to fit down in my own

skin for a while, single-minded as a surfer. The first
day here, there was nobody, from one distance
to the other. Rain rose from the waves like steam,

dark lifted off the dark. All I could think of
were hymns, all I knew the words to: the oldest
motions tuning up in me. There was a horseshoe crab

shell, a translucent egg sac, a log of a tired jetty,
and another, and another. I walked miles, holding
my suffering deeply and courteously, as if I were holding

a package for somebody else who would come back
like sunlight. In the morning, the boardwalk opened
wide and white with sun, gulls on one leg in the slicks.

Cold waves, cold air, and people out in heavy coats,
arm in arm along the sheen of waves. A single boy
in shorts rode his skim board out thigh high, making

intricate moves across the March ice water. I thought
he must be painfully cold, but, I hear you say, he had
all the world emptied, to practice his smooth stand.

Mississippi River, near Cape Girardeau, MO

My father and I take our usual walk
by Cape Girardeau's seawall that steers
the river as fast as possible past us,
from Minneapolis to the sea. The wall's
spray-painted with messages of love and hate
along the river side. And with eagles.
Some skill went into them. One perches,
a Harley-Davidson logo, brand name below
the sketch, the other bird in full flight,
and under it, Isaiah: "They shall mount up
with wings as eagles." Some Huck Finn, here,
still shakes off the weight of widows
and deacons—Oh motorcycles, wings, rushing
water! I have not had freedom in my life.
Crossing these granite rocks on shore,
I think, now, at this age, how it would be
to kill the wild pig and light out in a canoe.
Those on shore could bury my memory.
It would do no good for my father to weep.
The long river would dash me to the Gulf,
where the land would open its hips
and I would float into clarity and a sweet
brine. The water would turn to sky.
My canoe would be a smile, and I would
paddle from island to island, saving lives.

Mother of the Bride Dress

I'm walking around the outer roped-off
circle of Stonehenge, considering whether
the dress I've ordered for your wedding is
after all exactly what you want me to wear:
it's aqua, several shades lighter than
the teal blue you said, with beads on bodice
and sleeves. If I were a pre-Druid woman,
entering this dread eclipse between the henge
stones, the color of my dress would hide me
in the sky. I would be beady sky, leading
you. You would look like swallowed light,
and all around us the silence would be filled
with distance, and sheep. My shoes, dyed
to match my dress, would punch holes of sky
in the grass. In these ancient rituals, all
existence wants to face the sun! The way
not to disappear, dear one, is to start talking.
Once we entered the inner horseshoe of stones,
I would tell you everything about the past. By
the time the final blows of sun landed
on the bluestones, I would have you caught up,
at last. We would look at each other
in elaborate detail, laugh like temple bells.

St. Paul's and St. George's Church, Edinburgh

I choose this shell of a church because I want to see
what God does when He lasts more years than people

can afford. It's an ordinary parish church, but large,
its tympanums and gargoyles drying out, holding on.

It is Sunday morning. On one side of me, a man sits down,
turning his gap teeth my way, wafting his body

like a thurible of cheap wine and bitter old human smell.
A woman slides in on the aisle side, pinning me in,

almost touching me, her face all one scar, vacant
from this angle as a half-moon. Her eyes sink

to asymmetrical wells, her hair floats in patches.
Under her warped mouth, another mouth, a smiling scar.

She sits against me in this vast space, a horrible
accident who probably can't afford repairs.

It starts up. The old man knows all the words and says
them every one off-rhythm. A hull tender to the quick,

the face of the woman knows how to be exactly itself.
What am I? A child. Nothing but a child,

caught by my own grace, my own new smell. And here
comes God, creaking down the nave, level-eyed.

Farthest North Southern Town

My hairdresser Frank's own hair's cut punk
today, livid as a ruffled bird.
He tells me about his brother-in-law
on the police force who tells him how
the cops punch out the punks on Main Street,
and get away with it too. They got
these leather gloves, he says, with brass
inside, so no bruises show, and even
if there are some, they're gone
by the time the trial comes up, or the judge
will say you might have fallen down
stairs. This town is the farthest north
southern town, Frank says, switching scissors,
and nobody wants to argue with the mayor,
who appoints the police chief, and so on,
like a ricochet bullet, down
to your basic level of cop who takes
his shift to count the number of times
the same car cruises Main Street
in an hour. Three time's the limit.
Then out he comes, cruiser flashing
red and blue. They mostly nail
the ones with racing stripes and mag
wheels, not the little Subaru wagons,
Frank says, spraying mousse in his palm,
lifting my hair to an elegant panic.
We are squared off in the mirror.
What's more, the law says they can still
hang you here, he goes on, for stealing
a horse. I won't, I say, I won't.

Burdett Palmer's Foot

You spend the night trying to dodge
patches of wet soybean meal that smell
like shit. One of the things you smell, though,
that wonderful wood, coming out of Natchez,
going north. But there's the soybeans,
the boxcars full of fishmeal, and chemical
cars, leaking gases. I'd work all night
with the lantern, checking cars and contents,
then the light would start coming up
behind the shapes of flatcars, wood cars,
boxcars, tankers. About five, I'd stop
at the beanery under the railroad bridge
for chili so bad after a while it was good.
The morning I saw the foot, two boxcars
stood misplaced in front of the beanery,
a crowd around the shoe, beside the rails.
They said Burdett stepped between the couplings
just as the links pulled tight and sliced
the bottom off his foot. Everything stayed
put, waiting for inspectors out of Chicago.
I was only seventeen, so I had to stick
my nose in the shoe, to see the private insides
of a foot. Burdett Palmer's foot, that
stayed too long in the same place. I needed
to see it close, and then I needed the long
sight north, a mile down track where the light
came to a point. Overhead, the huge arched
bridge left the boxcars and beanery as long
as it possibly could, before coming down.

Kitty Hawk

Man is not a bird, Wilbur observed.
The trick is to give up flapping

and rolling your own body
between the wings. You must

lie still like a cripple
and trust the gears to warp

and rudder the air
for you. You must work the levers,

give over to your intellect,
rise to objectivity, let the roar

of the motor carry you
up like a surf in your ears.

There you are, going against
everything you believe in—

the Church of the United
Brethren, a whole testament

of necks falling limp
as Sunday chickens, crazed skulls,

your relentless mother
waving her polka-dot handkerchief.

You let the great winged
wheelchair grind you across

the sky. To someone standing
off, *hosanna!* you are a white bird,

a shudder, running out of ground
the way the dead shall rise.

Anhinga

The anhinga is spread on the bush
like a rag, drying its water-soaked
wings. It must have just gone under
for a fish, and now it takes
a long time in the sun, snaking
its neck to smooth and pick its oil-
less feathers, one by one. We get tired
of waiting to see it fly. In all
that time, a purple gallinule steps
from lily pad to lily pad, four turtles
drift underwater. Behind the anhinga lies
pa-hay-okee, the river of grass.
Haven't you ever longed for preparations
to end? Did the anhinga ever actually
break the water? Sometimes even
the real world is a park where nothing
happens, but you think about what might
happen. You walk the paths, barely
able to contain your wish.
The animals turn away into their
peculiar shapes. This is what makes you
start telling lies, waving your hands
to illustrate, wagging your finger,
as you leave the anhinga for dead
with its hundreds of feathers.

Bombay Hook

Out of a great breathing emerge
winged things, a leafing, a shaping, a gathering.
Purple grackle crouch thick as leaves
in the trees. Then at some faint twinge

in the fabric of the day, they're wings—
a black rage in the sky. They're all
like that: starlings like schools of fish,
darting and swarming; thousands of snow geese

lifting and dropping to the ponds in waves;
even the lone marsh hawk, glinting
like a huge butterfly, buckles to wind
inside a faultless curve. Before dark,

low tide gathers plovers and pipers
dipping into the muck. The sunset sky
turns restless and winged: so many nights
in the world, who could count them?

The one breath keeps on like a sleeping child
under a down quilt, turning by the will
of a dream, or the twitch of a muscle that knows
what it sends away, and what it holds.

FROM *BREATHING IN, BREATHING OUT* | 2002

Fourth of July Parade, Albion, WA

Everyone's happy, catching candy.
There's an army truck, one fire truck
screaming, a blue Olds about 1975;
two police cars side by side,
everything huzza-huzza;
the band playing "From the Halls of Montezuma"
from a flatbed truck; eight kids on bikes,
with balloons; a dozen 4-H kids in clover shirts;
a bulldog with a bow;
two hefty rodeo girls on horses;
a small tractor pulling prizewinning chickens
in their two festooned cages.
I can't help it, I get sentimental tears.
Damn, I say to myself. Chickens.
A prize for being chickens.

Then, amazingly, here they all come again,
back up the street, chickens
from the other side,
fiddle players instead of horns showing,
candy flying again like stars.
Everything a copy of itself, another chance.
Quantum physics says it's true,
particles coming and going.
The road not taken may be taken.
Meanwhile the chickens move forward
again in our eyes, the Declaration of Independence
gets signed. We need custom,
return. We like to sit sandal-footed in the grass,
happily surrendered to either side.

Past or future, it's no wonder
the chickens win, the way they keep
their artist's eyes cocked, lost in the work
of being chickens
        again and again.

Buying the King-Sized Bed

I am already thinking of rolling around that expanse,
tossing a leg without entangling. The way I am,

though, I see all the possibilities for loss. I see us
pillowed and billowed, supported in exactly the right

hollows by ergonomically designed, pocketed coils,
while beneath it all—the pea under a royal height—

the oppressed, the downsmashed, sleep in despoiled
cardboard boxes, or three on one frayed blanket.

Think of us, spread out, tongues on the rampage,
marking where we'll kiss. Oh wild God, how can

you permit this excess? How could any of us gauge
the exact distance at which people turn strangers

to each other? In our double bed—called double,
but we have been bumper cars and cliff-hangers

on it for years, our shorter ancestors troubling
us still—I can't even raise my knee

without poking my dear love in the groin.
We have been close, we have understood each

other the way people in tight houses start growing
into each other—at a molecular level, absorbing

each other's pheromones. Yelling and slamming doors,
too, or else they are lost inside each other! They would

have grand houses, if they could. They would forge
on like Jet Skis through the foyer and out to the good

sea. They would send a wire to say, "I still
love you." The sweet old world is longing to be

loose and light. All night long it stares up at the chilled
stars. This is a sticky business, finding the peak

distance for love, knowing our bodies will be nothing,
someday, wanting to hear them make their delicious,

reassuring sounds, bobbing against each other.

Cosmic Pitching

Fidrych would lift his wild golden curls
and talk to the sky. Hrabosky the same,
and he'd talk to the ball, circling
the mound, face twitching. And then he would
face the centerfield fence, whirl back
around, go into his stretch, and
pitch.
    It's best not to take chances. You
get your mind stalking and empty.
You slap your glove on your thigh, pace
your pattern. You make a ring of not-caring
around the thing. Too much pressure on one
point and the energy's down a black hole.
Carlton, on the watch for UFOs, what he might
have been doing is picking up an
archipelago as it moved through its
calculations. His mind was just breathing
in and out.
        So much that's far-fetched
lodges between the in and the out.
Did I mention Luis Tiant, flinging his
head to the sky as his arm came down?
Proof that the center of the world is in
the body, not the sight. You get these actions
together that don't care about each other.
They don't stand for anything.
        Listen, ball.
Bless you, ball. You and I, ball.
You get into a rhythm. Inside the rhythm
is a pitch. You keep your mind on the
rhythm, waiting to feel the pitch coming on.
You don't know how to speak directly to
the thing you want more than anything.

Somewhere

I am all right. Everyone else is out there
crying and going on, but I have gotten
in here with my nice dead grandmother.
They have her on a gurney, legs
sticking out of the sheet, the red stem
from her thigh to the canister
on the floor.
        Getting her ready for the
funeral, honey, taking the blood out.
We're going to put this clear stuff in
before she's cold, so she'll be beautiful.
Already she is, clean as stone.
I am all right here. I am happy
enough in her little room with the
smells, even after the scrubbing.

        My hand on her arm, so they
have to say *dead* again, and they say it
exactly the way I knew it, something you
check out and pass on by, dead
robin, dead rabbit, dead worm, nothing
to turn back for but a kiss
on her mouth, which is flat.
        She can't feel that, the one in
suspenders says, *but somewhere, she knows.*

Somewhere begins separating itself,
stretching itself into the field
behind the house, into the tall
grass, the things to be found
in it—the mole holes to China, the zillion
little stone eyes of Africa turned up
to me. I am holding my

breath between continents, while she lies
pinned to the center, wearing
her glasses. If I stretch out my hand,
the air is a faceless body
and I am standing here
like a dumb bunny with my hand, pulling
it back into my memory.

Dogs

I am off for my walk along the shore,
a cold and windy day like the one Elizabeth Bishop wrote about

in "The End of March," the sky the same mutton-fat jade,
even if I don't know what mutton-fat looks like.

I remember she was following dog-prints big as lion-prints.
The biggest dog here is Josie, more like a barge

than a lion. She limps arthritically up the street,
eternally optimistic. Amanda and Dewey disband their symposium

so everyone can kiss each other in secret places.
Then the Lab with the red bandana comes up.

Then I come to the three full-sized poodles, teeth bared.
The white one has gotten out of her fence and starts

after me, red bows bobbing over her ears.
I don't know why I can't just walk down the road thinking

about how Elizabeth Bishop turns her sun into a stalking lion.
Probably it was a shadow. I feel a little responsible

for the animals, I pet them when they let me.
I do it in memory of my poor brother, and Mrs. Laverty,

who taught him the 300 words before he died, and I do it
in memory of the yelling and sobbing. I could just as well do it

for Elizabeth Bishop, opening her eyes, trying to remember
what to be ashamed of, how many words

betrayed by drink. I try to remember her poem, the animals
shadowing me, stammering and practicing,

breaking my heart with what they can't say.
Their faces are like boarded-up summer houses, canny

but withdrawn. When I look at them directly, whichever dogs
have come along dubiously nose the ground. And sometimes

I wonder if they should trust me at all, the way I get lost
in Bishop and her lion and mutton-fat jade

while the world around me is
slurping and sniffing with recognition and pleasure.

Highway 5

We take the direct shot
instead of the coastal route,
not being able to have
everything, of course.
None of that entanglement:
fantastical ruffling of bays
and inlets, little houses
with slammed doors, gravel
driveways, faces with
three days' growth of beard.
This bleached line singing
like an aria, not part of
the general narrative.
Like a neutrino beamed
through everything without
flinching. Ah, to travel
light as light, to hold to
the straight and narrow idea,
to take the wheel and—
as if it were a museum
cross-section of a giant redwood—
draw a straight line
from its center: "Magna Carta
Signed. Columbus Discovers
America. Civil War Begins."
There goes our personal
will, petty prejudices
elegantly tossed off behind
like Isadora's scarf.
There goes this difficult language
dashing like wild horses
into its heaven of metaphor.

Where we're headed, the setting
sun's a long-stemmed rose
held out before the eighteen-
wheelers: THE END, backlit
pink, a campfire in the dark.

The Poet Laureate Addresses the Delaware Legislature Opening Its First Session after September 11

Naturally we go on, even though the great
double watermark stands behind everything now.

Even this poem—if you held it to the light,
you could see the Towers shadowing behind it, their steel

beams bare couplets of moonlight. How free
this poem might have been, I like to imagine,

if the Towers hadn't shaped it. How free the air was,
before its division into good and evil, before

the planes, before the law of gravity. What law
could we possibly have passed to keep the air from leaning

one way instead of the other? Here we are,
in Delaware, a breath south of New York: whatever

shadows the City, surely shadows us.
And, too, we have these eroding beaches, poultry

manure greening the bay, houses spreading
across the broad expanse of farms. Still,

here comes this poem, setting up its boundaries,
its own little rules, trying to start over, to be

the kind of poem even kids can say by heart.
It wants St. Georges Bridge in it, arched like a dolphin,

the C&D Canal gleaming through it like a crack
in an egg lit from the inside. It wants to be the kind

of poem with snow geese lifting off from Bombay Hook.
Word by word it starts building itself out of nothing.

It listens to its heart, the encouraging beat of its heart's
own law, law, law—except for

that double shadow, that one missed systole,
diastole—and then again the blessed law.

Rumors of Changes Circulate on Penguins

On the island, you have at least
Dostoyevsky, the Bible,

and penguins, a trembling sea
of penguins, an ice-floe of waddle,

alert in their water of thoughts.
It is an island of flat-footed

parents and children
caressing each other with their

noses, playing at likeness and un-
likeness. They angle across

the ice the way I do across this
page, dear one, a little wavery

from the tears in my eyes.
Things will change, I write

to you. Look at the way your grief's
in motion already, a little island

of sociability. I am awkward
writing it, but I keep hoping to

build momentum, get the words
to start blackening the shoreline.

And don't you have
the classics, sort of a general

history? And the penguins,
all cocking their heads as if the

air were magnetized? You could
watch the way they try to catch

which sounds they should
turn to, in the circus of sounds.

Cow Falling

There is a story of the crew of a Japanese fishing trawler picked up at sea,
who claimed their boat had been sunk by a cow falling out of the sky. It
turns out they weren't drunk. Russian soldiers had stolen a cow out of a
field and for a prank had loaded it on their transport plane to take back to
Russia. But the terrified cow dashed madly back and forth, banging into
the walls of the hold until they decided, for their own safety, they had
better push it out over the sea.

The cow that jumped over the moon
drifts now like a table down—
not drifting, really, but ripping along as if she had been shot
from one of Monty Python's catapults, hysterical bulk,
udder waving in so much brooding space
she appears to drift
toward a rippling plain below.
As the sun strikes her, she lights up, a Golden Calf now,
an astrological sign, an advertisement—Elsie the Cow—
if the fishermen would look up.
But they are preparing the trawler like a manger for the event,
coiling ropes, pulling in nets.
They are passing over the surface, oblivious
as the clipper in Bruegel's painting,
while the heavens are opening,
while the cow lists temporarily to the side, feels the sag
of her body, watches the only sky available
in the last, interesting minutes—
though it is all the same, clouds or plains of water,
rolling across her vast mind.
Now she herself is rolling for no reason back to her feet
above the widening black craft where the Japanese fishermen
are hauling the last net in, laughing
in their small brotherhood of hunger and smells.
The cow falls heavy and heavy,

monotonous and unromantic, part of all things falling in nature.
At the last second they see her as she sees them,
each uselessly drawing back in mute recognition
before the shattering, the counter-idea,
which is definitely wrong in one sense and regrettable,
which could be, though, exactly what the gods intended,
another unusual birth and death
of a few moments' duration, to be believed or not,
an ancient Chinese koan
to drive the thinking mind out of itself
to rest on the fluctuating sea.

Spring

As soon as I start to pay strict attention
    to that white lily diving upward
like a ballerina, naturally

I look up and there's a man on the trestle,
    studying the murky water.
I have no way to gauge

the exact depth of his misery. Maybe
    he's thinking of jumping.
I could be recalling yesterday's *Oprah* show

about the man who jumped
    and only one guy in a whole crowd
tried to save him,

too late. Though when I see him there,
    even in my imagination,
I wonder if it's my ex-husband, always

on the edge of a cliff, or a trestle,
    smoking a Tareyton, thinking he'll
jump. How no one could save him,

but my brain keeps ledges he can quietly
    sit on for a while.
This is what I'm used to: the one thing

like the sweet uplifted arms of the lily,
    and then there's the other. Neither speaks
to the other; there's not much to say.

They could be dancing the tango,
    eyes outward into space,
moving as if the other's only something to

maneuver with, to keep things going.
     But it's spring, so
let's say the man on the trestle's remembering

his daughter's twelfth birthday,
     when she asked him to dance with her
in her new ballerina slippers.

When I said "ballerina" in reference to
     the lily, he thought, instead,
of her skinny beauty, before she took the job

at Burger King and gained the weight
     and moved in with her boyfriend,
although these days he feels lighter,

released from her life, a little.
     And she's going on a diet, quitting
smoking. This is what spring is like.

In the grass by the lily, a worm's
     probably opening little breathing tubes
in the earth. The man can

sit up there all day, breathing. He can keep on
     looking like a leftover hippie,
pulling down his dirty Dodgers' cap.

He can keep on, without me.

Leaving Lewisburg

      Under clouds, the Juniata River's pewter,
pitted with eddies like an old mirror.
I'm slipping along
thinking of a person's reflection
worn away. I don't like to keep
saying good-bye, with all this moisture
and springtime. The churches are looking
upward and downward, but I am thinking of
how fast insects fly, how they create
their own vortex of air like a tiny tornado,
always on the verge of stalling out,
but they don't, because the outer tip
of the wings moves faster and throws air off
the end. Very ingenious.
Horseflies can copulate
in the air at ninety miles per hour.

      Probably things that seem mysterious
have simple explanations involving
engineering, luminous and metallic
as the Juniata. I drive alongside the river
almost to Harrisburg,
thinking now of huge gray catfish
underneath, mopping their whiskers
against the mud, creating their own map.
And then a line gets pulled, the fins open out
like kites, the mouth gapes like a huge
bottle opener! It may turn out to be nothing
up there but one small johnboat, a simple
period. But suppose that period
were an insect, with oars for wings

and could take me anywhere.
I wouldn't want to leave for another world,
but keep on straight along this one,
that would turn out cleverly
to be everywhere I go.

Mary Rose Quotes James Joyce
on the Cliffs at Bray

We are chuffing along in our heavy shoes,
watching a scene on a nearby peak:
"She's sitting on his hips now,

running her hands up and down his chest,"
Mary Rose says, as if I couldn't see, myself.
Martello tower's across, and the house

of that terrible Christmas dinner
in *Portrait of the Artist*. Mary Rose quotes
the beginning: "Once upon a time, and a very

good time it was." We recall what followed,
the tears for poor, dead Parnell,
for the abused stones of Ireland, the very same

stones that young woman braces her feet on
now, as if to say, "What of it?"
Here we are, clumping upward, across

from the pearl-pale seemingly quenchless lovers,
seaweed masses rocking below.
It all feels out of hand: Joyce's Christmas

gone haywire, politics tangled with the mother's
breast, the breast of turkey, the wine,
and now this ecstasy near enough to touch,

the whole universal exclamation thrown upward
out of the mind. "I could never, there,"
Mary Rose says, and I agree,

but the scene is working in us, a pebble
in the shoe. From the beginning, sure,
we had hoped to be loved without conditions

until we cried out among the seagulls.
We are quiet now, we know exactly
what we are up to, we are busily wrapping
the lovers in layers and layers of language.

Sunday Morning

They are miles out in the country, so you will have to
imagine them at the glass-topped table, having their oatmeal,

watching the awful house finches fight at the feeder, squirrels
gathering up the scattered seed. She tells him about the Copper

Age Iceman in *National Geographic*, the oldest intact human, 5,000
years old, dug out of snow in the Italian Alps. She describes

his body, lean as a jackal, flesh sucked against the bone, his
face dark and a little moldy but still entirely covered by skin.

"He looked tense on the snow," she says, "his hip torn by a
jackhammer, his genitals broken away." They watch the finches.

Her husband asks about the jackhammer, and the genitals.
"It was a policeman who did it," she answers, "thinking he had

a newly dead man to pull out." They talk about the blundering
human race, as people do in the complacency of oatmeal and

oranges, before they start their day. The husband is thinking
about his Baptist childhood, the sin of the world placed on his

small heart, and the Iceman's hip crushed like a bird's
wing. He wishes the Iceman had been left under the glacier

holding his precious packet of cells. "They're afraid of
being alone. That's why they dug him up," the wife says, slicing

her orange. "We keep longing to find our old selves still under
the ice while we've gone on inventing cars and airplanes."

"But what will happen to him now?" he asks. "Behind glass,"
she replies. Their separate thoughts converge at the glass

and look in. The woods are bright as glass, after the rain.
The closer they look, the more the Copper Age man breaks up,

like a newspaper photograph at close range. In town, other
people are at church, singing hymns. If you could get to a point

as high as God, the man, the woman, and the congregation
would turn into dots, just the same. You would miss the wife's

hand coming to rest on the husband's knee like a blessing.

Chicken Bone

I can almost see her
rolling her eyes, trying to
get her breath, my father
coming behind to do the Heimlich
maneuver in Mrs. Pete's restaurant,
Mrs. Pete herself—she of the
$4.95 dinner, dessert included—
stepping in to do it right.

Before this, what?
They are talking about the heat,
maybe, the grosbeak
on the feeder, the rusting screens.

How long could that go on?
The menu could take a while.
A missing earring.
This is the way they
spend their lives
in our absence, this and
The Young and the Restless.
"I'm finding out what makes
the young restless,"
he says.

We children and the soaps,
swarming around their chicken
and mashed potatoes
like starved ghosts,
while they behave politely
to each other, God knows,
charity and violence having closed

together above them like
a little tent at last: the third
thing they've refused to speak
of, the limit to everything.

Guess what they do
now? They figure the tip
on a napkin, not one cent
extra for the life they're in.

Hyperspace

Tree trunks seem to keep shrinking all winter,
and by mid-March the Elk River's visible in blips

from horizon to horizon, when the sun's going
down. Some things I want, I only get a glimpse

of. Coltrane at his gentlest—you can still hear
what's harnessed, though. He might be playing "Soul Eyes,"

but it's not just eyes. His sax is opening its
mouth like a hole in space. I have the theory of a

net laid across as a kind of protection. It is like
latitude and longitude, or more abstractly, the warp

and woof of belief, the kind of thinking that
separates day from night, heaven from earth, and so on.

Suppose the universe began as a tear in the fabric
of another universe. On a two-dimensional plane,

the tear would look like a pushed-out curve
the shape of Coltrane's saxophone. What if there are

ten dimensions, and Coltrane is in the three
of space and the one of time, and the rest are hidden?

They might be quivering out there like branches
of invisible trees, or wormholes in the branches. This

is a very religious feeling, beyond belief. Not
everything is vertical or horizontal. I keep thinking

I should do something instead of just stand
here, it is all so beautiful for the few minutes

I can see the flat plane of blazing water
through the trees, and the terrific sun on the brink.

Language

One day Adam said "Adam"
and found out he was standing

across the field from everything
else. It scared him half to death.

He lifted his arms as if they
could help. The air felt cool.

So he said "air" and "cool":
a population of not-Adams

sprouted everywhere. One
of them was Eve, a wild card.

He heard her clearly, distinct
from his internal voice, his

private naming. She was singing,
"In time, the Rockies may tumble,

Gibraltar may crumble . . . ,"
and sure enough, it was

something o'clock already.
He saw that her mouth was pink.

"Pink," he said, because it was
small and had lips to push the air

away. And there was something
else, he was sure of it, a softening

of the air between them,
a spell. Nothing could be the word

for it. He was reeling
with the wound of it, the chink

between subject and object.
Light entered, memory followed

and began to tell its own story.
He felt himself held in it,

traveling *within* it, now,
driving toward a particular town.

"Something's happened,"
he said to her, but she'd guessed

the doom of it already, the wooden
signs along the highway

bravely standing for everything
that matters: *Burma Shave,*

*Kollectibles Kottage, The Cock
& Bull.* She ran a finger delicately

along the window as if she could
trace what it was that had

broken loose from the two
of them, that was running crazy

out there, never looking back.

Chat

The absence of chat bothers me
every winter. If one word can get away
like that, I begin doubting everything.
I was trying to get to the library in Fayetteville,
grinding chat under my feet up Dickson street
(trying to get to the real library, not the bar
by the same name), and that was definitely
chat heaped against the snowbank.
Small particles disappear, then it's easy
to slip, an armload of books skidding
halfway down the block. I remember
the block where I knew all the names: Bauder,
Glenn, Adams, Craig, Stevens. I know
these were right, before they died. Now
all the rooms have been redecorated.
I wonder if I'm okay. I get the entire
Arkansas Highway Department fixed in my mind,
the men finishing their cigarettes, saying,
"Load up that chat, we're spreading chat
today." Chat is poured into trucks.
The men have no idea of the circumference
of their world. They think it goes on forever.
I say *chat* to the people I know here.
They've never heard of it. Things in my past
might not have happened. My first husband
laid his hard hat on the table. I'm not
sure if I was there. I look up *gravel*
in the dictionary. I look up *chat*, which is
only a verb. I feel a little guilty,
filling in where nothing exists. When my
father is talking, I still have to work hard
to get a word in and make it stick.
When my mother is talking,

I have to find a word, put it in her mouth
and let it rattle around so she can make a sound.
I am almost crying, trying to get her to say
anything. I describe the absence the best
I can. A man and a woman are on opposite sides
of the street, calling across. They have had a life
I don't know, I can't even hear them, in my car.
Two trucks in front of me are full of chat.
I take it as a sign I should write this.

For the Inauguration of
William Jefferson Clinton, 1997

Not having been asked to write the inaugural poem,
even though I am from Arkansas, I will take what's here,
the birds at the feeder, not saving the world but only
being it, each kind of bird taking up its career

to fill out some this-or-that of creation on a small scale,
like this poem nobody asked for and few will hear.
Cold birds, eating extra for warmth, finely detailed
to catch the sun. Ridged out in friction gear,

they jerk from position to position, as if the eye's
first impressions have been caught before the brain
smooths them out. The chickadee clamps a precise
seed and tosses its shell, nothing amazing.

To start up a fanfare would be to see it as specimen,
to deflect one's attention from the exact life performing
its dip, crack, toss. The long beak of the wren
is extended by a thin white stripe traced full-swing

down the head, so the wren seems half beak. I need
to get these lines, delicate as a Chinese painting.
Any poem would quiver with delight, with the chickadee
in it, or wren, but wouldn't want to do anything

about it. That's the hard thing about writing a poem
that's supposed to inspire the country at a crucial time,
that's supposed to hammer like a woodpecker. No one
could hear, with its hammering red, black, white!

It doesn't bode well for the quiet poem, or the insect
inside the bark, or the old tree crumbling to dust
inside itself while the public word *tree* holds it erect.
Still, I think when the bleachers no longer rise august

along Pennsylvania Avenue and the meandering ocean
of confetti has been swept up, it is good to cross a bridge
in your mind, to something earlier, oblivious to emotion,
something like wrens going on inside the language.

Your Body

I could trace everything: where you're
soft, where rough, the taut and slack
of your body I know in the biblical sense.
I could describe all that, call it metaphor
for the inscrutable, and embarrass you
standing here in your bones, covered
by your black pants and shirt, your successful
tie and suede jacket, professorial yet
a little rakish—a good and lyrical surface.
I could deconstruct you in front of everybody,
point out your internal contradictions.
Your bald head and hairy chin could
stand for the more complex issues.
I would circle you like the blind man
describing an elephant, making the error
of parts, while you head on out the door
like Wallace Stevens, keeping his
private and cryptic language, never a word
of family, never an allusion to poetry
at the Hartford Insurance Company.
I can hear your body being that quiet,
modest, only decorative enough to affirm
our mutual taste.
            God, I don't know,
I just wanted to say something in *honor*,
and it all looks so confessional.
The body is what teases me, Eliot
in his banker's suit, fingering his spectacles.
Williams returning from rounds,
shirtsleeves rolled up to reveal hairy
(or not) arms. Bishop, stepping out
of the tub, a few rolls at the stomach,
a little too much weather around the eyes.

Dickinson, pacing her room,
thin white underneath the white—
but secret thigh muscles, powerful
enough, I imagine, to keep all that grace
under pressure.
       Happy, angry, or sad,
I am utterly drawn to this mystery, as if
it were the magnetic center of life, a pole—
oh, and then the Freudians will start in
on me, with their connective tissue of prose!
Memphis the cat is kneading my chest,
press-press, press-press, her eyes blankly
earnest, mouth watering. She doesn't
give a hang if I'm her mother or an iconic
stand-in, it's the flesh she loves under
my sweater, the body of my body of work.

I Write My Mother a Poem

Sometimes I feel her easing further into her grave,
resigned, as always, and I have to come to her rescue.
Like now, when I have so much else to do. Not that

she'd want a poem. She would have been proud, of course,
of all its mystery, involving her, but scared a little.
Her eyes would have filled with tears. It always comes

to that, I don't know why I bother. One gesture
and she's gone down a well of raw feeling, and I'm left
alone again. I avert my eyes, to keep from scaring her.

On her dresser is one of those old glass bottles
of Jergens Lotion with the black label, a little round
bottle of Mum deodorant, a white plastic tray

with Avon necklaces and earrings, pennies, paper clips,
and a large black coat button. I appear to be very
interested in these objects, even interested in the sun

through the blinds. It falls across her face, and not,
as she changes the bed. She would rather have clean sheets
than my poem, but as long as I don't bother her, she's glad

to know I care. She's talked my father into taking
a drive later, stopping for an A&W root beer.
She is dreaming of foam on the glass, the tray propped

on the car window. And trees, farmhouses, the expanse
of the world as seen from inside the car. It is no
use to try to get her out to watch airplanes

take off, or walk a trail, or hear this poem
and offer anything more than "Isn't that sweet!"
Right now bombs are exploding in Kosovo, students

shot in Colorado, and my mother is wearing a root beer
mustache. Her eyes are unfocused, everything's root beer.
I write root beer, root beer, to make her happy.

Einstein on Mercer Street

While a student at the famous Polytechnic Institute at Zurich, Albert Einstein fell in love with the only woman in his class, a Serbian named Mileva Marić, who at first was able to keep up with his mind. They talked physics and declared they'd never settle for a bourgeois life. Their first child, Lieserl, was born before Albert decided they could marry. They either gave her away or she died. Nothing is known about her.

They had two other children before their divorce. By this time Mileva had given up her career and had sunk into a severe depression. A few years later Einstein won the Nobel Prize, and—even though he was married by then to his cousin Elsa—he sent Mileva all the prize money. Twenty-three years later, after Einstein had become a U.S. citizen and a professor at Princeton University, the United States dropped the first atomic bomb on Japan. Einstein had nothing to do directly with the development of the bomb.

1

Ah, Mileva, it's always you I turn to
    in my thoughts, on my walks down Mercer Street,
lone old lump inside my gray raincoat,

the parabola of my felt hat.
    They keep me like a Kubla Khan
at Princeton. My floating hair they talk of:

His floating hair. Beware! Beware!
    Weave a circle round him thrice.
Reporters flash in my face. Even the bomb,

they claim, was my idea. One marketable God
    of the Intellect, they want. But what they catch—
each shot's a different man.

Put them together, flip quickly,
    and I'm still, I swear, the man you once
thought: a motion picture, a wave, a music,

a disturbance in something else. In you,
     maybe, as you are in me. As if I'd never
left you. A man never loses the woman

he has children with. Even dead.
     It's the hope—what we thought we could be—
that hangs like a moon

over the field of my losses.
     Oh my Dollie, my schnoxel, this is your
Jonzerel-silly-names, fastened to you

by my nerve endings. We were going to fly
     so far outside the gravity of the bourgeoisie,
we would remain all thought, wit, music—

eternal students, the "we" of significant work,
     ein Stein, one stone. Then it all felt like stone.
Now I talk to myself.

2

Still, somewhere inside the so-called ether,
     I feel you listening—dark, peevish
as always, your intelligence rasping like wire

against mine. Somewhere I'm still
     playing Mozart—in spite of you—half the night,
a fool for him, and Bach, their harmonies,

their unfailing return after infinite variations
     as if the starting point were all time sucked inward,
or some anthropomorphic God were calling

eternity back into this intersection with friends.
    Three Divertimenti: clarinet, piano, me on violin,
the children asleep, you my angry Mileva

curled in shadows, what we each called love, I guess,
    the mathematics we made of our marriage,
against the emptiness.

3

It appears that the universe bends toward
    itself, a geodesic dome,
two hands, fingertips touching like a person

in thought. If I moved faster than light, I could
    draw the bow back
into the music's mouth, rewind data.

Never allow, for instance, that monstrous
    nuclear heartbreak, *not* my invention—
it was the math that got pushed so far

off the edge of reason.
    Where were you? Turning back, giving up
your books, no longer able to follow me.

4

Rewinding: Up through swirls of snow, switchback
    turns, precipices, up to Splügen Pass.
You brought opera glasses

and my blue nightshirt. Heads touching as one,
    we studied a snowflake, fractal,
circular. At dawn we sent snowballs down the slopes,

imagined the village below, avalanched.
    Always we had to oppose, to disturb!
The disturbance of pregnancy, then:

our atoms inexorably carrying on.
    I withdrew, as I do, to follow a thought.
Even then I guessed the extremes things could come to:

the snowball chain of split nuclei
    that can start forking through plutonium,
doubling, quadrupling from one generation

to the next in millionths of a second, releasing
    matter back to vast, primordial energy
you can never put your hands on again.

5

I thought I was a pacifist. Good work needs
    a certain peace. Ah, then Lieserl—
we agreed, didn't we, what to do

when she was born? So as not to undo
    the future. (Who knew then if we'd ever
marry?) "As what do you have the child registered?"

I had to know that, at least. To be a Jew—
    another strike against her. You think
it's peace you've won, but sometimes

it's only quiet, while the violence grows,
    a snowball chain where you can't see.
After the boys were born,

Lieserl would knot and twist
    in my troubled stomach: this cramp.
Every day it feels as if I'm giving birth.

The doctors say drink milk and more milk.
    I wanted peace, so I could think.
This is what I get.

And in Germany, Hitler rose up
    like all my dreams of deformed children,
children sinking in the waves, children lost.

6

    I note the universe goes from order to disorder,
        yet it remains. With my own eye
    I saw a man fall from a building

    into a rubbish heap and live.
        The man said he felt no downward pull,
    which made me guess that we ride along

    inside our own frame, you in your truth,
        me in mine. Why did I have to wear socks,
    then, to please you? Because of a universal

    fact: mass can't help but bend toward mass.
        I like only shoes, these two boats
    that keep me pretty much afloat

    by themselves, an elegant sequence, like notes.
        Take Mozart: his perfect symmetry
    that gets where it's going. But there has to be

    someone outside the music, to listen,
        for it to break the heart with joy.
    Who else is left to listen to me, old enemy?

7

    Since Elsa died, I'm down to
        Chico the dog, *Tinef* my sailboat—
    worthless thing, but a pleasure—

    and this fame. If I could do it again,
        I swear I'd become a plumber.
    The mind can't stand too much pure thought.

It oppresses. You oppress me
    still, my dear, forever brooding.
Things ought not *be* all probability. This

will make you mad: I told Elsa once,
    "If you (meaning her, of course)
were to recite the most beautiful poem,

it would not come close to the mushrooms
    and goose cracklings you cook
for me." Plain things, like sailing.

I can sail now like a swan. I like to be
    carried along, making calculations,
but I admit, truth's not ordinary:

it disappears as soon as you look.
    It's like catching the wind,
trying to make it bend to fit your mind.

8

When I was a schoolboy
    in the Alps in the rain
at the razor edge of a cliff,

among small black birds,
    when I slipped
in my poor shoes and was barely

caught by a classmate—
    what do you think
would be the mathematics of this?

Since a person freely falling
    could go on forever,
and it's only the sudden embrace

that holds you here,
    or there, how does one
show up at the coordinates

on time? Were we at the right
    place, or wrong,
my little veranda, my Dollie,

my little street urchin? We did
    save each other once, I think,
and once is all there is.

IV

Tillywilly Fog

I'm kissing his poster, on my knees on my bed.
We're both children, in a way. Maybe we stop
at fifteen. We could easily be in the fogged-
up car at Tillywilly Quarry. We haven't, you know,
yet. It begins here. The rest seems like a vast
openness. I cannot imagine past his hand

up my skirt any more than he could imagine handing
back his songs to silence, or lying on his deathbed
without Priscilla or Kathy or Linda or Jo or vast
numbers of other girls called in to stop
his mind enough so he could sleep. What we know
together is half-shut eyes, call it a fog

of desire, if you want, but there is something in the fog
that is not us, an alertness of mind, a hand
running over the entirety of what we know
and calling it good. No matter whose bed
you get in later, something in your mind stops
here: you and Elvis touch lips across the vast

distance. Don't sap this up: the truth is vaster
than the jewel-belted icon stumbling in a fog
of barbiturates. The vibration of the universe never stops.
It's all song, the hum of molecules in the hand
and lips, and what goes away comes back, a flower bed
of humming, spilling over the edge of what you know.

You think the fat women who cried didn't know
what they cried for when he died? It's no vast
distance between them and me. Our souls are bedded
in our hungry bodies, taking advantage of the fog
at Tillywilly. "Please let me put my hand
there," he says, and being scared, he stops

there. Nothing ever felt this good, to stop
on that note, the mouth wide open, no
thought left, no design, waiting for the hand
of God to move on or intervene. It's vastness,
it's plenty, it's human spring, pure song, a fog
of wastefulness. You get out of bed

the rest of your life knowing it's Elvis's bed
you've come from—vast, vibrating. On the one hand,
you're stopped, flesh and bone; on the other, you're a song.

I Escape with My Mother in the DeSoto

Listen, it will be all right. I'll drive. Good-bye
Maxwell Street, we'll say as if we had a secret
emergency, good-bye Bendix spin-dryer, good-bye
petticoats on the line dripping liquid starch.

What's the right phrase you've been looking for
all these years, spitting your morning phlegm?
I think it's *Fluid Drive*, that revolutionary automatic
kick of the DeSoto into third gear at 45. Exempt

at last from the science of shifting that makes us
both weep! I can get this thing up to 70, flat,
in the stretch by the agri farm—
used to scare starlings out of trees doing that.

They lift up now, brittle as leaves as we pass,
get past. "Your Father—," you start in as if he were
in the trunk, but then you open a Pepsi. We are
watching him dry up and die away like an argument.

You have worn your pink flowered shorts
and it is as cool as the basement on a hot day,
and Arthur Godfrey has not yet fired Julius La Rosa.
It is as if we are down there listening to the radio,

knees pulled up on the brand-clean chenille bedspread.
We are going through *Ladies' Home Journals* and you
are a beauty queen, safe in your vault of clichés,
safe from having to explain anything you mean.

Elvis Aron and Jesse Garon

"When one twin died, the one that lived got all
the strength of both," their mother Gladys liked
to say, and that remnant of a son would pluck at her voice,
the little dread in every pleasure, and Elvis
would quiver on the stage of her thoughts, and she would kiss him
on the lips, and he would kiss her back, and let her
take him to her bosom until it felt like the other son
joined with this one, and Elvis could leave her again,
carrying the seed of worry and decay away
that never had a voice. On camera, then,
he would seem to cock his head to listen,
shock of hair over one eye. He would take
Dolores Hart into his arms, and we could almost
hear the dark child sigh in its dream of being born.

Memphis Discovers Elvis

She hears her son's name
over and over, "That's All Right"
played eleven times.
Memphis sits by the radio
while he's gone to see Autry
in *Goldtown Ghost Riders*.

If you're going to have a famous son,
you already know before it happens,
but still, it seems as if they're saying
he died, instead of what they do say—

this boy who used to sit on the curb
at the corner of Main in a sailor hat,
bright and earnest, but oh!
the city flinging itself into him even then.
Who could say when the awful
moment would be, when the child
would step off into one particular song
as if into heavy traffic?

Too late to save him now.
Gladys and Vernon rush down
opposite aisles of the movies.
Nothing to do but get him out of there
and down to WHBQ.
Tell him the disc jockey wants him
to recall as best he can
his mortal life, on air.

Elvis Goes to the Army

"Good-bye, you long black sonofabitch," he says
to his limo as he climbs on the bus to basic training.
The U.S. Army has him on the scales, then,
in his underpants, baby-fat showing, mouth downturned
in sorrow or fear. It is worth noting when a person
chooses to leave his mama and his singing behind,
gives over to the faint signals picked up by his inner ear.
So what if the signal in a particular case is mundane:
the unremarkable desire for clarity, for love.
He's more alert than he's ever been, time clicking
away with the greater ritual's small appointments:
dressing and undressing, tightening bedcovers, reciting
the valuable gun, becoming part of the diorama
where danger is everywhere, a good reason to blend
khaki with the earth.

       Now, thirty years later, uniforms
are back in favor, following the lead of Catholic
children in navy and white, soldiers of God
and high scorers on SATs alike, sure
of their place in the universe. "This is the army, son":
even a King like Elvis might hear that
and relax at last between what's come before
and what will be: the dead hair of the past
buzzed off in a second, a battalion of stubs that hope
to live up to the example of the fallen. We will not laugh
at the shorn head but will consider a long time
the incomprehensibility of our desires and the way
we beg ritual to take them off our hands.

Shaking Hands with Nixon

Otherwise, Elvis would be crashing against
the walls of the Oval Office, confused bird
in silver-plated amber-tinted designer sunglasses
and purple cape,
high-collar shirt open halfway to the waist.

He is trying to get things under control.
Joplin and Hendrix have just died of drugs.
Uncle Johnny's died of drink; Cousin Bobby's swallowed rat poison.

Elvis has brought Nixon gifts, a fistful of deputy badges
from his personal collection
and a picture of Priscilla and Lisa Marie,
even though Priscilla's just walked out on him.
He has come to ask Nixon for a Federal Bureau of Narcotics badge.
He has done an "in-depth study of drug abuse,"
particularly among Beatles fans.
He's worried about the Beatles making all that money and
taking it to England.
He tells Nixon they may be un-American.
He tells Nixon about his gun collection.

He tries to get across that he knows the awful changes
the country can make when you're not looking,
how one moment can desert the other
and leave you standing in the footlights,
trying to remember if you're supposed to shoot or fly.

Sputnik, 1957

Remember the upswing, the peak of the swing
    from the catalpa tree where your stomach paused
        in perfect equilibrium
between thrust and gravity? To get that far and hold it

all around the world, to orbit like the Russians!
    In retrospect: to keep being ten, before,
        well, you know
what followed, what junior high was like: the cold mornings

when your little Silvertone clock radio clicked on
    a moon in the still-dark sky you had to enter,
        both feet
on the cold floor, one foci of the day's ellipse,

of the fancy bluffing you practiced how to do
    out there, the other you still holding on,
        cold feet slightly
turned out, a hard little bow of feet. The world

split into here and there. Remember, too,
    your Vassarette training bra, your awful
        tantrum, the way
you threw it across the room after one day's

straitjacketing? How loose the Russians had gotten,
    you thought, how lifted, how barely held
        on America's string!
How definitely you would rather be Red than Dead.

Elvis Sings Gospel

The picture of Elvis late at night at the piano,
singing gospel. Everyone has left. There are a few
folding chairs and the upright piano. Elvis
is lifting almost out of his black-and-white shoes;
there's no music to look at. It's so simple, the way
loneliness sits down in the middle of a bare room
and the middle gives way, and here you are, in the real
music that meant itself to be played. He is leaning
to the keys, bringing them to whatever the point was—
the typical point of getting washed in the blood of the Lamb,
or building a sure foundation, or going home
to the Lord—but he is hearing the words as exactly themselves,
individual, no reference to anything. I am not
imagining this. I know it: the way the words
save you by themselves, the hush of the word's entrance
like a spirit-lamp. Nobody wants anything
more than they want *home*—what *home* means—
struck like a gong against itself, reverberating
Gladys, maybe, or Uncle Vester, the Assembly of God
Church, Mississippi Slim, Big Mama Thornton,
Ernest Tubb, all the way out to the barely audible
crowds, the great weariness to come. But inside
is the word, encouraged slightly into music, taking
the shape of the room until neither one exists
anymore, doesn't have to, since it is home already.

Industrial Teflon Comes into
Use for Kitchen Pots and Pans

After the wars were over, the ones people sang about,
things quit sticking. My grandparents, for instance,
shook the dirt from their shoes and moved to town,
drove the paved streets of Columbia, spurned
orange juice for astronaut Tang.
And what year exactly did I start shaking off hugs?

For a wedding gift, I got Teflon pans.
Teflon, if you'd like to know, is a long-chain polymer,
a fluorocarbon plastic, like Freon.
As good as gold and platinum at resisting things.
Eggs slide right off, as on TV.
Not to mention what came after, Reagan and Bush,
facts sliding across the screen, disappearing
out of memory.
Not to mention the literary canon: Pope, Richardson,
Dryden, Spenser. Who reads them now?

The private name he used to call me, what was it?
The last time, he came through snow, bringing
a bottle of Mateus, and we made love
on the floor, not looking at each other,
nothing left but flesh and bones.
It was 1973, still no news of the danger of Freon.
All summer, I kept the air conditioner on.
The kids opened and closed doors, hot and cold,
the holes in their hearts forming already.
Surely my own mother must have held me, early on,
before I recognized her broken heart and turned away.
Surely her own mother must have held her,
sometimes, in spite of garden-smudged hands,
just to hold her.

Bus Stop

You are scratching your foot
against the steel leg of the bus seat,
imagining yourself a woman free on the road,
cornfield after cornfield.
You are seventeen and returning to the town
your father's failure took you from,
returning to your old boyfriend
to tie things up so tightly
a whole lifetime cannot untie them.
You picture him encased in his Buick
like a dark spool, his mind turning over
and over, winding you toward him.
After dark, though, you let your head droop
against the soldier from Chicago
on his way to Ft. Chaffee. He
and his friends speak softly, the click
and mumble of their voices naming
guns and machines while you lean on his
khaki, move on out with the infantry,
face the open-mouthed cannon

which is only the neon flash
of the Iron Skillet bus stop in Centralia,
where you and the soldier are sitting
on stools, smoking and talking over
your separate futures as if the talk
were already betrayal,
your heart lurching awfully easily
into this happiness of riders, his pale mouth
at the center. You hunker
in his mouth to get near your heart.
Out there someone looks up—a small, wild

dishevelment. It is your reflection
in the bus window. You are back
on the bus, are you? All right, then.
you curl up alone on a seat, stuck with
your original plan, too dangerous
a person for anything else.

The Night before Her Third Marriage, She Watches a Rerun of Elvis's Comeback Performance

The night before her third marriage,
she arranges flowers, watches reruns:
he forgets "Heartbreak Hotel"—clutches

his throat. "Worst job I've ever done,"
he says. She loves his failure like she loves
her own skin. She loves his fear,

his one-of-a-kind black leather jumpsuit
over it. She loves whatever protection
there is. Elvis reads his cues

aloud: "Things to talk about"—*First
record, when first met musicians,
Ed Sullivan Show, shooting from waist up.*

Pulls his finger over his curling lip.
While he has her laughing, he's gradually
relaxing away from the past, toward

where he is now, the stool he's sitting on.
He's closing his eyes, going on
with the songs, courting the front row.

She watches for the moment now,
knowing, from the future, how backstage
after the first set, he called

the costume designer to dry out
the inside of his suit, which he had come in.
She wouldn't want to say how hard she's

watching to see the moment of coming.
He jabs his hand straight up, shouts
"Moby Dick!" and spears the whale. *Now.*

Or when he leans into the girl's face as if
she already planned to leave him,
so he sends her all he has. It would be

something, to catch what was missed before,
to get in sync with him. It would make
a kind of opening between them, through which

you could fill the past with shaken blossoms.

Elvis Acts as His Own Pallbearer

Life up to now had been no mistake,
getting out of East Tupelo,
out of the sharecropper's shack.
Fame was nice.
But this is America,
where you keep redeeming yourself
by leaving the past behind.

It wasn't him in the coffin; anyone could tell
it was a wax dummy. The hair was coming loose,
nose too pug.

How many times had he disappeared
like a magician?
He used to get the body shaking,
the left leg wiggling,
then half-sneer, turn away
from the audience as if he were kidding,

as if he were shaking them off.
We saw how it was done.
You had to make up the moves every day
of your life, start over so many times
you were obvious,
completely American, almost invisible,
so you could leave again,
carry yourself out to the garden
and see what came up next.

Mrs. Louise Welling Spots
Elvis at Harding's Market

I felt like I was seeing fireflies—getting little glints,
you know, of what's behind the regular.
Maybe it was the rivets on his suit,
the sunset beaming in the picture window of Harding's Market.
I was standing in line with a full cart,
ice cream for my grandkids, bread for the freezer, etcetera.
He was in front of me, head ducked under,
hair flopping, paying four dollars for fuses, I think.
He had on a white motorcycle suit,
helmet on the counter.
I've never been much of a Elvis fan,
but when you see someone, you know who it is.
Nothing to say about it.
What would I have gained, saying anything?
Put fireflies in a jar—you've got bugs
in a jar, dull tails flashing now and then.
When you drive down a road, though, through fireflies,
they look like an eye opening as you pass between.
I wasn't surprised he was alive.
My nephew getting married—that surprised me.
But Elvis—once a person's all over in movies and records,
I don't think he knows when to stop.
I wouldn't go for a ride on his motorcycle if he asked me.
But when I came out and he was gone, my feet hurt
and I felt tired, useless, like I've always
been going toward something I can't ever get to.

I Visit the Twenty-Four Hour
Coin-Op Church of Elvis

—Portland, Oregon

Well, sure, it's only
a window in a brick wall,
and eight small, seven large, circular framed Elvis-faces
that spin when you put fifty cents in.
The computer screen asks you what you want: wedding,
confession, or what.
I got my personal Elvis ID card:
The bearer of this card is a SAINT in the Church of Elvis.
He or she may also be Elvis. Please treat them
accordingly. Thank you.
The faces were spinning like 45s
and I was combing my hair in the plastic reflections,
fixing my lipstick. It was a subtle change.
I think I am probably Elvis. I have begun to feel like
a lost child in Portland, anyway,
to feel uncertainty about my life,
to feel a religious determination to make my words sing.
I was crossing Banning Road to meet you here for lunch,
keeping my hips loose, my sunglasses on.
Didn't I order a cheeseburger for the first time in years?
And I feel I am gradually being purified
of my irony,
back to the true rock and roll.
I want to run my fingers through what hair you have left
and call you Baby, throatily,
and mean for you to Treat Me Accordingly.
We could do our wedding vows again.

I feel we could get all the way back to the original vows,
before our separate cosmic fractures,
the vows we made years ago to other people
that had no irony whatsoever,
that were all Love Me Tender, all Heartbreak Hotel.

Elvis Reads "The Wild Swans at Coole"

During the First International Elvis Conference in Oxford,
Mississippi, Elvis, alive as ever, is asked to read aloud
"The Wild Swans at Coole," to see what a Hunk

-a Hunk-a Burnin' Love could do to expose the other,
more subtle, longings to the average citizen who might
be raised to contemplate a little, for God's sake,

instead of falling into a blind beat, producing unwanted
babies and maudlin tears! Elvis fingers the page,
tries to plan what to do, sick to death without the music's

jingo, the strings that drive it, and the lyrics that fasten
to the music and ride on through, so the body can be
the words. Meanwhile, they wait for their poem.

He starts at the first, trees in their autumn beauty,
nine-and-fifty swans that take off, or don't, so what?
Among the rows of wan faces, nothing for the thoughts

to take off on, nothing to ease the thoughts. Poem
clamoring on instead of a song, words that aren't supposed
to be said southern, lines that end before you're finished

thinking, and the last question breaking through the levee
at the end of the lines. He thinks what to do, then, with
his naked and weightless body. They are listening as if

they had got the secret of life into the poem, now,
even with him flying off the end of it, trying to swagger,
one hand in his pocket, bravely cocking an eyebrow,

off into the wilds where the girls are screaming, wanting
his babies, no questions asked, ah yes, the subtle grass
of the wilds, and the drum-beat of the human heart.

from "Graceland"

Elvis's Bedroom

They have a velvet rope across the stairs.
I have to leave him alone up there,
dreaming trompe l'oeil clouds on the hallway
ceiling, dreaming his bedroom blue,

"the darkest blue there is," dreaming black
furniture. Leave him in his midnight with Jesus
on the easel by his bed; pass by the upper
landing, raised like hairs on my neck,

like a few bars of music climbing
and dissolving in front of me. Leave him with his
sleep-mask on, windows blacked out.
Leave him in his giant quiet, his woman

or no woman, his restless sheets. Go on
with my tour, go on convincing myself
that if I were allowed upstairs, I'd retrieve
years of my life, that I could walk in

on the years so quietly they'd let me sit down
and think how to live with their hard facts.

Lisa Marie's Favorite Chair

Lisa Marie Presley spits her peas
into the wastebasket, knots up like a pea
in the fruitwood jungle chair, "so big that a window
had to be removed to bring it in,"

Priscilla says on the tape. I know
how she curls to abandon the world, the kitchen
voices. How you climb down the chambered nautilus
of yourself, room after room. How the first dream

you have is a flicker of light on a curve.
You could name it Michael Jackson because
it is a cool dancer, pale-faced, androgynous:
perfect mother and father, not

breaking plates in the kitchen. You watch
your supposed love-light dance, refuse
to be caught, flare cold as panther eyes. In your future
of dreams he breaks free from a dense upholstery

of jungle leaves. You can never touch him.
Your factual life diverts, trying. You think
you're going straight, but then again, you're here.

The Mirrored Stairwell

There she is, dozens of her in unison,
stepping down to Elvis's basement pool room,
stepping through her multiple facets down
to the original, who is stepping onto the now-extinct

running board and into the Ford forever,
not dancing to the radio but climbing in
deliberate as an old woman, gathering her skirt
before the age of jeans, gathering herself

for the long sleep of sex, the ragged
lawns of Garland Street strewn behind her,
the music inside the houses stuck
the way music stays with the insane,

or people with Alzheimer's: "Mack the Knife,"
"Venus," "Lavender Blue," "Teenager
in Love," "Come Softly to Me," and so on.
Beyond the Ozark Mountains, Alaska and Hawaii

become states. Nixon debates Khrushchev,
Castro takes over in Cuba. She steps
into the car as if into church, the closed eyes
of the center, the dark from which things wake,

if they can, if they sense the slightest break.

The Meditation Garden

You're supposed to think on something
by the curved brick wall with Spanish
windows, cupping the two steps down
through Roman columns to the graves

where Elvis, Grandma, Vernon, Gladys,
and Jesse's little marker fan out
like bracelet charms below. Signs
of presences stand everywhere. Jesus

stretches out his arms to St. Francis
in cowl and hood, to a black river goddess
and a white one with an Elvis-nose.
Cherubs bow their wings. A naked

blackened angel holds an empty pot
beneath his arm. No one knows
what lives inside the hollows of this world,
lip-synching from the other one.

Might as well include a pantheon
of gods, the whole shebang, just in case.
No sign's trivial: *Aaron*'s engraved
with double *a*'s on Elvis's grave.

If he were really dead and buried,
the story goes, wouldn't they
have spelled it right—with just one *a*?
Didn't I believe Whitman when he said

"look for me beneath the soles of your feet"?
Didn't I believe the former husband
who said "I'll haunt you forever"? But one
positive note: I've kept singing the old

songs in my lousy voice until they don't
even recognize themselves. And who's
to say who's right, with all the cover-
versions since? Whose song

would you say "Blue Suede Shoes" is,
for instance, Carl Perkins's or Elvis's?

V

If Names Started Coming Loose

Cow, for instance, might hook itself
like a horseshoe around a fencepost.
Chair might land on a cat, try to
assimilate. *Chickadee* could shudder
loose, to discover itself staid, roomy,
with a two-car garage. The ones
left behind? Vaporous, probably
afraid, not yet knowing how to live
inside discontinuities. Meanwhile,
cow would quite naturally be grafting
itself as efficiently as possible to
the fencepost, upright, unflinching,
drawing no flies. Like the rest of us,
it would be willing to go for a small part
of the truth, a little more onomatopoeia,
a little less floating. Try to think of it:
your name, the one you've repeatedly
handed out to strangers, now landed,
say, onto the huge steel patio grill.
"I'll just throw these burgers on the
Maryann," someone might say. And you—
the you that's running on empty—
would be moving like a rumor among
named objects, not unnoticed entirely
but treated with the maneuvering
of the other guests who know they
must know you but can't quite
recall . . . Makes you want to hang on,
doesn't it? It does, me. To admit to myths,
vow beliefs you never thought you'd
settle for. That's the part of you that
wants to live inside mere obedience
forever, place the salad fork on the outside,

pass the potatoes clockwise. But then,
suppose there's the lightness beginning
to come on, incredible continents
inside you, rising and breaking apart,
the voice you never knew was yours.
Suppose it's so good it has no name.

Biology Lesson

Ontology recapitulates phylogeny.
I love the sound of that,
the way heredity's an automat
set on a repeat serve. Compulsory

rhyme, I'd say. I say it now,
thinking of the pit to China
we dug that summer in Nina's
back yard. It was our upside-down

doubles we were after. I think
of us digging past lunch,
past dinner, skinny and hunched
over that yawning, impious link

to the underworld. We were like
the buck I saw yesterday
in my path that outstayed
me: concentrated, in love with might,

maybe more with fear. The hole
could go on forever, we
could come out feet
first on the other side, the soul

of us yanked like a radish by some
bathrobe-wearing, slant-eyed
devil. We would divide
from our old selves, a martyrdom.

We would be born again.
Again, we would start up
with our plan to interrupt
the plan. It would be our discipline.

What It Was Like

My mother dragging the vacuum cleaner like a large cockroach
room to room. My mother folded like a moth, sitting on the stoop.

She's not crying now, she sips her Pepsi through a straw. She's "mad,"
she says, as if it were only a bug in her throat. I grow alert as a deer.

I grow aware of bad local grammar, hoards at the gate. I roar off
with my friends down Dickson Street, bringing civilization to Arkansas

in someone's T-Bird. Some conglomerate picture shifting as if
underwater, not that, but a womb-thickness. I push through, assembling

as I go. I wish I could hold onto my mother's feet, very small and white,
high-arched, ticklish. Her feet only, far enough from her eyes.

Her eyes in my memory: one brown pupil off to the side, trying
to escape, the other dutiful, their hopeless drama. Don't look at them,

but at the mottled pattern of the linoleum countertop, the flared
aluminum legs of the dinette, my rage equal exactly to my love, two

pistons. You ask me what I remember: I'm halfway up Mt. Sequoyah
on the other side, gasping for breath. I turn to catch the long Ozark valley,

the glorious translucent yellow of maples. I'll call it mothering
because of the way the land and sky hold you, and at the same time

lay a hand on the back of your neck like a dangerous lover.

Fayetteville Junior High

What happened was, when we weren't looking
Mr. Selby married Miss Lewis.
We tried to think of it, tiptoed Mr. Selby,
twirling the edges of blackboard numbers
like the sweet-pea tendrils of his hair,
all his calculations secretly
yearning away from algebra, toward
Miss Lewis, legs like stone pillars
in the slick cave of the locker room,
checking off the showered, the breasted,
flat-chested. All this, another world
we never dreamed of inside the bells,
the changing of classes:
Selby and Lewis, emerging
from rooms 4 and 16, holding hands
like prisoners seeing the sky after all those years.
"Bertha," he says. "Travis," she says.
The drawbridge of the hypotenuse opens,
the free throw line skates forward,
the old chain of being transcended
in one good leap, worn floor creaking
strange as angels. In homeroom, the smell of
humans, rank, sprouting, yet this hope for us all.

Knot Tying Lessons

The Slipknot

—the most useful temporary knot or noose.

What can I say? I turned a corner. No matter
that I doubled back, there was still progress. I was lying
low, crossing under both my coming and going,
and when I rose to see where I was, felt the cool
air on my face, I skidded like a skater, wrapped around
myself again, burrowing back up through the small
figure eight I'd made of myself. How secure it all seemed,
how sure to result in something unfaltering—patriotic,
even. But the way things have gone, I'm left with
a looseness through the center.
There's been this tendency to let things drop.
It's the opposites I have trouble with,
the way my attention begins expanding as if
the richness has eased past the borders, no longer
lives in this constriction, this lump in my throat.
I drew you to me with such firmness, you were sure
of the implications. The exact point at which I began
to be disappointed, who knows? The more I gave myself
room to work it out, the more I felt the movement
of possibilities within me. I should have felt relieved
when all fell through, but I only felt what I am,
how I'm made. "Open your mouth," my mother used to
say, coming at me with a bar of soap because of some
word I'd said. I opened, as I do now, willing to take
the bitterness, to have done what I did.

Makeup Regimen

I've developed complicated pores, I need radiance, more beauty steps,
more ice-colored bottles, the old me exfoliated so the young one can emerge

dewy, daily. As if I could see my own face, as if the mirror reflected me
by the shortest route instead of at crazy angles, all probabilities adding up

to my face, as if it weren't our ignorance that makes things appear in their
classical forms. When the Newtonian God went away, what took His place

acts more like rain, mist, sunshine, bounded by horizons du jour. Enter
clarifying lotion, like the crisp, high range of stars. The face of night's

supposed to be naked and spread from ear to ear, but at dawn the workmen
arrive with their electric saws, their hydraulic hammers; everything's to be

built again. The sum of it is complex: for example, my mother's mouth
when she died was all wrong. They made her look mature, confident.

Their mistake was concentrating on the flesh, trying to fill the emptiness
with it. She had her red suit on. They took her jewelry off when all we asked

for was her ring, leaving her not quite put together forever. I like to think,
though, that dying is like falling all the way back to where everything's

held to itself by memory. Two old men I knew in Arkansas would pass
each other Mondays on their country road, driving so slowly they had time

to ask after each other's family. "Mr. Caid," one would say, and nod.
"Mr. Kimball," the other would say, and nod. The main thing was to come

along looking as much as possible like somebody same as the week before.

Mouse

I admire the way mouse dashes across the top bracket
of the blinds while we're reading in bed. I admire the tiny whip

of its tail at the exact second my husband tries to grab it.
I admire the way it disappears into our house and shreds various

elements. I admire the way it selects the secret corridors
behind cupboards and drawers, the way it remains on the reverse

side of our lives. The mouse is what I think of when I think of
a poem, or of music, going straight for the goods, around

the barrier of our thoughts. It leaves droppings, pretending to be
not entirely substantial, falling apart a little here and there.

Clearly, it has evolved perfect attention to detail. I wish it would
concentrate on the morning news, pass the dreadfulness out

in little pellets. Yesterday I found a nest of toilet paper and
thought I'd like to climb onto that frayed little cloud. I would like

to become the disciple of that mouse and sing "Wooly Bully"
in a tiny little voice in the middle of the night while the dangerous

political machines are all asleep. I would like to have a tail
for an antenna. But, I thought, also, how it must be to live alone

among the canyons of cabinets, to pay that price, to look foolish
and trembling in daylight. Who would willingly choose to be

the small persistent difficulty? So I put out a spoonful of peanut butter
for the mouse, and the morning felt more decent, the government

more fair. I put on my jeans and black shirt, trying not to make
mistakes yet, because it seemed like a miracle that anyone tries at all.

Trillium

—named for its trinity of leaves, of petals.

The universe prefers
    odd numbers. It leans,
        obsessed with
what's next. It likes syllogisms,
    the arguments of
        sonnets: if A
equals B, then C.
    The ground-level
        common denominator,
the blood-red whorl
    at the base, is not
        an answer but
a turning. Does that leave you
    dizzy? What can I
        say that would
reassure either of us? Even
    our prayers have to
        catch hold
as if we grabbed a spoke of
    a merry-go-round and tried
        to convince
the universe of what we want
    stopped, reversed.
        What it gives us
instead: this bad-smelling
    beautiful bloom.
        "Let go, let go,"
is what it says, and who wants
    to hear that?

Small Boys Fishing under the Bridge

—for Josh, Zach, Noah, and Daniel

1

I watch them try and try for nothing
but tiny bluegill, sunfish, crawdads even,
anything to feel a tug, though they'd call it
necessity, as if they had to feed a dozen mouths.
They bend over the night-crawlers
with a whopping knife, too jagged, in love
with tools, machines, reels.
They're serious, removed, all of them,
threading half-worms as bravely as they can,
leaving me out of it, trying to act as if
the oozing is normal, required, after all
they've been taught about kindness.

2

It's excitement and mystery under here,
a boat churning through, echoing against
the bridge, and Zach, pulling up his bluegill
at last, shining and flapping.
He stops its fins down with his fist.
The fish looks at him, one eye at a time,
from its other world. From this one, the meaning
seems clear: the yanked hook, the yellow
plastic live-well barely wide enough for a fish.
But there's the human to figure in,
the complications of its mind, as it crouches
beside in splashed and sticky shorts.

3

After the hammer-blow, it's not so hard
to saw off the head, to scrape scales
into a universe of stars, fish-quivers
giving way to plain flesh.
What lesson can be learned by this?
It seems like no lesson
on the blue-willow plate—only eating
or being eaten, which turns out at last to be
a quiet exchange, nothing that could have been
helped, desire being what it is,
and fish like little knives,
pointed toward it all the time.

Light

I don't want to get started on such a nice night, but when I'm
standing out here and the security light's blasting from the boathouse
over the way, incessantly headed my direction
as light does across water and I can't see the stars only orange
bug-light and the nasty-wasp Jet Skis angled half out of the water
and who's going to roar off on them at night anyway and I'm
without the big dipper or the little or the entire dark past
or the crawdads under the dark, and even swimming nude
is problematical in that glow that's intended to mean I try to figure
what, *here we are in the suburbs*, maybe, *because the dark's
dangerous*, and me, I like to walk out barely seeing my feet,
just flicking on a light at the end of the dock, not to go
too far, and then when it's off I'm floating with only the upper
world breaking through in pinpricks we've given names to,
in our idleness or fear, but nothing like this tactless yowling
of light. Wouldn't you think there'd be boundaries, like when
a car drives by rocking with bass and I can't hear
myself think, wouldn't you think there'd be some respect for
people's secrets, invisible as they are, some acknowledgment
that the invisible's worth something, that I'm here, that there's a god
of some sort that picks up steam in the dark spaces, the more
dark, the more chance—so I try to turn my back to the light,
but is it awful of me now to remember Kraków, Kabul,
Monrovia, the yellow bombs in the night saying Kilroy Was Here,
to want to stand on this dock representative of my version
of history, declaring no more light, no more sight of Jet Skis
taking no risks with their noses in the air, wouldn't you think
the dark would finally get angry, at least in my lifetime,
and I could watch the retribution, the darkening, that the stars
would begin to reach earth with their clear messages, that they
would have something to say after all that distance about traveling
through their opposite, doesn't it seem reasonable that I would
want to stand on the dock and wait for them to arrive?

Ode to the Buffman Brothers

Timmy so big he's awkward as a loon on land,
    but when he gets on his backhoe
        and his brother Luke on his Bobcat,
you can believe we were born for machinery.
    They get the big maple ready to go,
        Timmy rubs the backhoe's neck
against its trunk, slowly up and down until
    it begins to crack, as we all would,
        and falls through a perfect tunnel
of trees, wild hair every which way, Luke
    scooping it, and the smaller ones,
        into the huge dump truck. Then
they really begin, Timmy with his delicate
    biting and scooping, clanging the small head
        down on the cement walk,
lifting a chunk to the dump truck
    like a dead mouse, Luke backing
        and twirling in place. They do-si-do
to the low rumble of motors. They come right
    to the edge of the house's foundation,
        they bite out a row
of stones around the old icehouse, they leave
    a perfect cliff, you should see it,
        roots exposed like the wiring
of the world, the smell of dirt and rocks and roots.
    Another thing: yesterday, they said,
        at six thirty a double rainbow
landed about here. They said it was a once-
    in-a-decade rainbow, and I missed it,
        This is what I mean about them,
what I can't get enough of. They make me
    want to start over from scratch.

Wild Lily of the Valley

Among the ordinary lilies
    of the valley, their bells
        lined up neat
as choristers, you're the country
    cousin, tiniest sparkler
        of bloom, stamen
projecting, nothing shy about
    you. And who isn't sexy
        under the trees
by the lake, who isn't
    a little aggressive,
        full of the need
to ignore the rules, to say
    something directly
        out of the thunder
of ground, the whole dark
    that spawned us?
        Nothing greater
than sex. The dark would run on
    forever without it.
        You show up
with your frowsy equipment
    powered by two clapping
        leaves, to unbalance
the civil town. Or, it may be
    my mind taking hold,
        tangling desire
in my hair until it is all a Medusa's
    coil, something we
        come to together.

No Heron

Herons are bigger than egrets, though they have the same long legs.
My father said one with an eight-foot wingspan flew over his boat.
I would like to be shadowed by something that big. It would seem

like poetry, just out of reach, moving and making a bare flush
of wings, and I would think of it long after, the way it was heading
away from me. My longing would not be satisfied even if I could

grab its scrawny legs in my hand, even if it nuzzled up to me.
I would be looking up the origin of *heron* with my free hand, and
when I read Greek, *to creak*, and Old High German, *to scream*,

I would wait for it to begin, but it would not say anything to me
in this boat which I am not in, but at my desk hoping for the heron,
a big one, as I said, so I can say, "Wow, look at that!" as if I were

getting up a circus. Out there are herons white and blue, not really
blue but smoky, with wings bigger than their bodies, dipping and
standing motionless beside lakes and rivers. Out there are universes

expanding until the space between atoms is too far to do anyone
any good. Thus, somewhere this minute one heron is calculating
the distance between his beak and a fish, the way it shifts. It is

as if he travels in space until heron and fish are swallowed into
each other. There is no heron at my desk. In fact, the absence
of heron is how I would define my study: no heron on the ceiling,

no heron on the floor, no heron on the wall, so that of course
I think of nothing but heron, how it floats its weight on one leg,
for example, flying that way even when it's not.

Knot Tying Lessons

The Perfection Knot
—a favorite loop among anglers, it has survived
the advent of slippery nylon monofil, which has
rendered many other knots obsolete.

How do we keep from going mad,
starting over with marriages and children,
making the same mistakes?
Over and over, we leave behind
the buoys that marked the shallows
we should have seen. They bob like zeros
behind us, counting for or against, who
can be sure? Maybe everything was
simpler than we thought from the start,
perfect as the disk of the sun, and the first
loop we took was never supposed to be
tied in some frivolous bow. Maybe
we were to come through the loop bravely,
cross its outer border until we could see
clearly how it was we began all this,
slip under what we used to think
was the route, until we caught
our waywardness in a noose, and nothing
could slip loose. Maybe it's the kind of thing
you have to teach your hands to do
without puzzling too much about it,
the way you faithfully get up, go to work,
come home. Like the rotation of the planets,
you have to believe that just because
no one says so, doesn't mean you aren't
okay, more than okay, really,
in your devotion to what you can't
exactly explain.

Knife

COACH CARS OF DAYS

Is the happy part days or moments later? Earlier? Things slide
through, a Metroliner of metaphors: Thanksgiving, Christmas,
bearing up against the sudden walls, tattered flags, truck beds,
concrete pipes, corrugated brown warehouses, silted ponds
with geese. Refuse and rust, the various ball fields, one game in
progress, its flush and fuss, no reference to us. On the train to
Boston for Thanksgiving. Or, all of us at the long table with the
china, plate after plate of shining destination.

A MOMENT SUSPENDED LIKE A PLUMB LINE

Over the motion of seasons, Thanksgiving and Christmas. Or
like a knife, or whatever is used to saw open your brain to go
after the tumor the size of a tangerine, caught in the crux of the
optic nerves, at the carotid artery, the pituitary. The delicacy
of this requires ignoring metaphor. Even though a person's
transformed—moment, moment, moment—the trick is in
keeping track. The trick's in staying with you like a surgeon.
I help you snap the flapping green gowns, one in front, one in
back. They put your clothes in a plastic sack.

THE AESTHETICALLY PLEASING SHAPE OF THE HUMAN BODY

The lesser is to the greater as the greater is to the whole: the
Golden Section: cross, crux, crucial, crucifix. In front of St.
Mary's hospital in Saginaw, Michigan, the statue of Mary stands
demure, bronze, encouraging. But high over the main doors,
she's art deco, almost gone already, refined to memory, an
aerodynamic flame.

THE UNFAITHFULNESS OF THE MIND

The way it keeps drifting up and down, forward and back, the
sign of the cross. Thursday, the night before, John made quattro
formaggi pizza. Pizza Giovanni, he said. This time last year you

were in Florence together. It's extraordinary, all of it, the pencil
point of a tumor you were born with, and now, its arrogance,
assertiveness. And the breath that's traveled though a corridor
so many times it believes it's entitled. As if the unimaginably
vast universe could agree to keep meeting itself like this!
Corridor. Corridor clicking along: door, door, door, a movement
like the bowels, the diaphragm, carrying us.

THE SPEECHLESSNESS OF THE SUN

Rising over the fields on our way to the hospital, huge orange
Midwest sun, spreading like butter along the snow-ripples.
Christmas lights still on, the shapes of trees and reindeer, those
night messages, even as the sun starts up again. I try to think what
the messages might contribute to the general silence. I can deal
with the painted windows of the hospital lobby—an angel on
a yellow star, dangling his feet, a pink-nosed mouse carrying a
spotted Christmas ornament, a yellow-chested penguin—because
of their obvious intention. The angel, the mouse, the penguin keep
trying for three and a half hours as we wait to hear from surgery.

SILENCE AS IF HEARD FROM THE END OF A TUNNEL

At the end of the tunnel, your shocked, quivering body, curled,
cut to the core, the ventilator, the mass of tubes. I know I'm
living right now, complexly, many chambered. I touch your
cheek, the you-and-not-you. The bruised right eye flowering, the
brain seizing, trying to steady itself like a small craft. How long
I have lived, finally to see how we can be ripped in a moment far
from ourselves. How time can be collected into glucose bags,
urine bags, potassium bags. I am touching your arm as if it were
our mother's arm, or my other arm, disappearing.

THE SHIFTLESSNESS OF THE LANDSCAPE

A couple more inches of snow. John has a tree sent, and your
sons and I hang every silly ornament, trying to get them right.
Your neighbors have tacked their usual obscenely pink bows

on greenery. What's been withheld, the garish, begins to shine forth, unencumbered. Thanksgiving to Christmas, the year moves to finish itself, its other nature.

A KNIFE PASSING THROUGH BUTTER BARELY DISTURBS A THING

The molecules part, the atoms steer their flocks of electrons to either side, like mother ducks. How spacious matter is, spacious as a laugh, the way it opens the diaphragm. Here's a joke: your head wrapped in gauze, tuft of hair, tube sticking out the top. You're a cartoon sick person! The tube drains off blood: ah, an escape route from the interior. I don't know now if we could have escaped our childhood after all, even though we tried as hard as standup comedians. Here are the smiling nurses, keeping the machines occupied while you go on getting away. When we came, it was just past Thanksgiving. Now it's past New Year's, nothing between.

HOW SATISFYING IS THE KNIFE, HOW PURE

I envy the knife; it is all performance. It has no interest in the infinitely slow absorption of blood back into the brain, the wheeze of the respirator. I envy the CT scan, the slices of brain back-lit on the screen in scientific portions so thin no one need feel sorry for any one of them. I envy the white areas and the gray, the way they keep their own counsel. I begin to suspect that days are a human creation, that the light and dark cancel each other out. To stand by your bed is to be nothing. Your tongue is a little bit out, your one eye a little bit open, but none of this has to do with you.

THINGS THAT COULD HAPPEN

(1) A nuclear bomb could tire of waiting. (2) Global warming could keep on melting the icecaps until a huge amount of methane gas is released that causes further warming, forming a cloud so dense as to block out the sun, causing a deep freeze. (3) High-energy particle accelerators could create hyper-dense "strange matter" that attracts nearby nuclei, thus growing larger

until the entire planet is compressed into a sphere no more than one hundred meters in diameter and rolls away under the bed like a lost nickel.

WHAT ACTUALLY HAPPENS

What actually happens when I speak to you, after the tiny bones of hammer, anvil, stirrup? After the internal seas, waving their twenty thousand cilia? What happens after their little electric jolts to the brain? What happens when I call the family, one by one, on my cell phone? Between the word and the word, nothing but radio signals. I could be saying a poem—who knows what happens out of sight between the words? And who knows if what comes up on the other side is past or future? I could be Jonah, trying to say something from here about fear and hope, those lozenges of abstraction, among the slippery fish belly ligaments.

CRADLE OF WORDS

Remember now in your sleep the prayers of various flavors of Christians, of Jews, of the one Muslim in the hospital lab, of Buddhists, of several atheists, in their way—the many who offered to carve for you out of the dark a bright cradle of words upon which you can be carried. *This one please carry. Carry on myth, on history. Encrust this one with our longing, with the magic longing calls its own. Saw this one in half and let her emerge whole. Through whatever narrow sleeve, let mystery fly out like a dove.*

THE CHEERFULNESS OF THE NURSES

The way they raise their voices as they come in, as if they wish to reinforce the need for living. Tweakers of tubes, adjusters of clamps and pillows. They flip the urine bag, they draw blood. They say only enough to maintain for the day, one day at a time. There's the Good Cindy and the Bad Cindy. One is clear, informative, exact; the other vague, unsure. Somewhere, the physician makes his rounds. Who wouldn't like to believe he's only a few floors away, coming this way, bringing a worldview, a philosophy?

SNOW

Falls, caked and heavy. Shadow, its acolyte.

THE BRAIN THINKING OF RETURN

Maybe it struck the brain just now, the idea of return, a kiss of electricity. Maybe the brain took a blowzy leap before it chanced losing its nerve. Or, maybe from the first breath of anesthesia, the brain's been plotting the landscape of return as strictly as a cartographer. Maybe the images the just-opened eye sees were first interior, moving outward, the difference between in and out not what we think but easier, more porous. The eyes open, they become yours, gradually, barely, brownly, from the blank world back, tiredly taking on their work. What an effort it is to *be*, to carve a clean line through the rubble.

TO THINK OF LATITUDE AND LONGITUDE AT THE SAME TIME

To place oneself deliberately in the crosshairs. To set a special table for Thanksgiving, to wash up, to decorate the tree and take it down. To light even these few fires that call attention, in the dark. *Holy Mary, snow queen, kite, flying with your flared bones over the entrance, I am having a revelation now. I imagine you making your choice.* "How hard things are, already, how seasonal," *you complain to the angel, but then you say,* "Okay, sure, why not have everything? Why not here?"

AND THE FORM OF THINGS IS FALLEN

Onto the bed, aching, onto the wheelchair, the walker, the railings at the toilet, the sitting up wobbling against the therapist, the slow clothes on and off, as demarcations. Flight with its maddeningly invisible wings marries the lumbering form of things and agrees not to give up, never to give up on each other, agrees to go home, to live in the same house, to eat Kashi together while listening to the morning news, to complain bitterly about the government, to hope for better.

Bladder Campion

They come in airy flotillas
        on each stem, little flower-
                blimps, propellers
of petals at their back ends,
        which makes me think
                how heavy with history
we are, and how alone, thus forgivably
        prone to personification
                of the gods.
We imagine the little bladders puffing
        themselves out because of
                their excellent
and homeopathic ideas, the barely
        earthbound kind that no one
                takes seriously
until they save the world.
        Every story we tell is only
                Horatio Alger, a pale,
yellowish and ordinary boy
        at the end of the row
                in junior high, who finally
amounts to something. A surprise,
        a profusion of campion,
                to demonstrate that
after the guns, the tanks,
        the barbed-wire we wanted
                so desperately to avoid
in our story, blooms will spread
        back across like plain,
                kind words.

The Death of Cleone

Of course she mistook
her son for her husband, since
it was the lake, and summer,
and she had grown small and turning,
as if the world were a kaleidoscope and she
its center made only of mirrors.
It was his voice, his hair, his height, so she
let down her own white hair and set her lips
on his before he realized. Still, when he
held her hand at the end, he was willing to be
anyone, and he talked to her of Central Lake
again, and when he reached the edge
of words, he took her arms
and made a motion of paddling
the canoe, and she did open her eyes
across the small craft of her bed, gliding
out into the last sliver of sun.
She passed the dam at Bellaire, through
Clam River, Grand Traverse Bay,
Lake Michigan, into the dream-soup
of details, of J-strokes. It was hard work
against the drag of water, before she
remembered she was a gull, and the water
turned to air. No, not a gull. Not that far
to go. Only back to Central Lake; she was
one of the ducks lifting off, pulling up
their landing gear in their awkward
duck-flurry of voices, and it didn't matter
which one she was, or who it was that
loved her, all of them winging around
within the hollow of the lake.
So began the silence, the evening,
the turning stars.

Poem for Our Twelfth Wedding Anniversary

I've lasted three days longer now than marriage number two,
a week longer than my number one. But the twenty-three years you

shared with your previous darling—I have a ways to go. Still,
we have to account for the way time compresses, distills.

We've been together barely 19 percent of your life,
now, 20 percent of mine. All that wake behind us, that strife,

it's as if we're wading through peanut butter. Neither of us
keeps souvenirs, other than our children, but every time you touch

my elbow, the inside of my wrist, I think of the difference. Not
think. The undertow of the past sounds a tone against that spot

like a temple bell under my skin. We're never entirely alone.
Let me put it this way: suppose we go to the matinee, our known

life left out there in the sun. We're ready to fling ourselves into
the plot, shed a few tears, which is the fun of it. Something new.

Then we're stunned by the inside light, made of all our infinite
remembered people and places, reshuffled to form this exquisite,

this strange tale. Sure, it makes us sad, or sorry, but the edifice
itself is pure bliss: all of us here, we're all caught up in the kiss.

Through Security

I take off my boots because of their steel shanks.
I take out my orthotics, place my coat and purse in the bin,
place my carry-on on the belt. I take off my shirt, my jeans,
my bra. I take out my contacts. I take off my makeup
and earrings, strip the dye from my hair. I relax my stomach
to its honestly protruding shape. Still, it's all over the TVs
about me. I'm buzzed again as if there's been no progress at all
since the club-carrying, the dragging-by-the-hair. I take off
my skin, veins flying like ropes, organs dropping away
one by one. I address the additional matter of bones:
unfasten ball from socket, unhook ligaments,
leave the electronic eye no place to rest.
I am almost ready to go, if I could quit
thinking, the thinking that goes on
almost without knowing, the tiny person
crossing her legs in the back
of the mind, the one who
says, "I still love you,
dear guilty flesh."

Lady's Slipper

Where are you going
in your yellow kayak
with your curlicue leaf-
paddles, your one red-flecked
petal-sail? How
will you get there
over the great fern-waves, under
the young maples,
the doomed elms?
I question your ability
to survive, this close
to the road in the
twenty-first century, but
the apparent ease
with which you've
arisen and blown yourself
into translucence
makes me think
you could go on forever,
after all, and alone,
making the cup
of yourself out of nothing
but loamy woods.
I recognize bravery
when I see it, the way it opens,
the way it enters itself
so that all
that remains is flower.

VI

FROM *LOON CRY: SELECTED AND NEW MICHIGAN POEMS* | 2010

Scavengers

They're out there rattling their trailers:
the pickers, the carrion birds,
bone cleaners, the shadowy
alley dogs, sniffing
out fish under the trash,
their sharp noses neither
moral nor immoral. Fiber
that moves through the arteries,
cleaning them out. I think
of Wilson, Lloyd George,
Clemenceau, after the Big War,
of the ducks dipping to the bottom
of the shallows, of the Romans after Greece.
Especially I think of the earthworms,
eating eighteen tons of debris
in a year; the ground full
of earthworms going at it,
extruding, making soil,
and of hundred-foot-thick glaciers
scraping it off, and of the sun
carrying off the glaciers,
and of combustion carrying off
the sun, and of death having
no dominion because
of the yearning that is always vast
and mysterious, a secret assignment
of the blood to find what it needs
(my items I left by the side
of the road—a rustle, and the rocking chair
gone in a half-hour,
the desk in an hour, wind

at the edge of a cliff, things
taken the way the breath
is taken), turning the body
back to before words
began to wound the silence.

Crouching

The day as nudging, as a nudging-stick, bark-stripped
and made to rattle across the storm drain grate,
hit the horse apples down, scrape along the sidewalk
and come, suddenly, to the deep crack, trace the crack
to its end, and the next, as if the cracks were a river,
a little portaging. There was no reason, no reason
to have a reason, and there was the creek that ran
over rocks for no reason, and the day opened
and closed like an eye to the ebb and flow of us into
and out of yards. I give her the name Sharon,
—not in the adult way involving exchange
of information, but of moving alongside of,
poking beetles to see if they move, the crouching.

Tragedy, then, more like a shadow, not
the dead baby robin in its half-embryonic whiteness,
not anything precise and possible to reach with the stick,
but huge and uncontrollable, parental. I want
to poke with the stick so that the hugeness will remain
in the upper atmosphere, not here where I am crouched.
What is the material at hand? The mink ate the baby ducks,
John Pixler killed the skunk and the raccoon. Light hangs
in the air after the rain. A man in Springboro, Ohio,
caught the record longnose gar weighing 14.72 pounds.
Did I mention that little glistenings have formed on the lake?
The terrible noises in the upper atmosphere are quieter
when I look into the microscope. There was all that
outside my bedroom door, and inside were the poems.

Hawsers

Things *must* return
from their journey outward—
the frayed ends of hawsers,
bones whitened and lightened,
feathers (bedraggled
is the only word for it, like a dog's tail
through mud)—
must return from the dolors
to their primary colors.
Humans have a stake in such
things—the eye's eye
with its three cone receptors,
the mind's eye that ties
everything up in three dimensions.
Sometimes, though, a small,
fish-shaped, slipping
curve, comes

Wild Turkeys

1

     Wild turkeys, necks jutted out, wattles flapping,
heads and bodies turning, all the same creature,
coming from somewhere, going back to somewhere,
ragged black and blood-red as if they were half-dead
already, chewed up. They remind me of Poe's bird:
ghastly, grim, and ancient, ugly as Roy Orbison
or George Eliot, ugly as Sir Robert Walpole, Lyle Lovett,
Eleanor Roosevelt, the ones who radiate ugly until
a person begins to lust after it. Lust like street kids,
pants below their underwear, hair screaming
bloody murder, shoving beauty out of the way,
as if the sonnets, the great waterfalls with their tropical
pools, even Britney Spears, were all distractions
from the fierce entropy, the smashed and flying glass,
like bits of bodies blown from tanks.

2

     The motion at the edge
of the woods is the turkeys with horny splay-feet
step-gripping with their sure knowledge
that the earth is what's moving, not them.
They're holding on with the purposefulness of the damaged,
the infirm, the wretched, who've put all their interest
into survival until they're lean, coded, all meaning
the same thing. I get this way, the old pain gone
but still on the edges, a damage of the heart
that doesn't hurt now, but knows what it feels like,
the turkey-head, the beak: the real things that went on,
the divorces, or rather, the agonizing over them,

my mother's death, or rather, the agonizing over her life.
It's the surroundings and not the thing, the ugly things
I've made out of my thinking, what I've hung onto,
my deep sleep of hanging on, while the wild turkeys
go on back and forth across the road, oblivious.

Deer

It was the deer. Or the raccoon lumbering away
from the feeder. It was America, pretending to be
innocent. I wanted to show you the deer because
we like to point out the wildness on our land,
as if the animals chose us from among contenders
for our purity of soul. The red foxes especially, the shier
the better, to show how far we are from McDonalds,
from Hummers. I wanted you to count the deer
with me, to agree that we love the world, the one
that can't be bought.
      Some days the sun disguises things.
What's missing out there burns in our eyes.
We rant about politics. We feel like survivors
from a dangerous life. We enter books, looking not
for foxes but for accurate punctuation, a good phrase.
We want to be part of something lovely. We love
the idea of deer—remember when there were twelve
roaming along the creek-bank in the snow? Maybe not
in snow. The snow stands for the page, how far
they have to travel to get here, how we can't
turn them away no matter what our hearts
are like, because of their alertness. We need them
for an alarm, for the terrible unnatural strangers.
The kids smoking outside the mall on a school day
are like those deer. They have muscles they might use
at any minute. They're perfectly made for escape.
      Meanwhile, we live with these windows,
this deck, and the wandering of animals.
We watch TV. It's ridiculous the way we sit here,

the way we talk, as if possibilities for relieving the poor,
stopping the war, were public, waiting, longing
to be enacted. Tails go up like flags. Under the tails,
the fierce smell, a dignity. Who knows what to do
when everything keeps so far from us?

Northern Pike

Just past the railroad bridge
over the Green River, the deep pool—
dragonflies and white moths—
where you can see the huge
fish hovering. And Zach
with his skinny arms, leaning,
and the whack of the line,
the wrenching. I wish I could
save him from his nightmares,
his waking fear of muggings,
of bombs, of what there is
legitimately to be afraid of.
Up came the pike, nearly three
feet long, teeth set on the line.
I didn't see this. Zach came back
with the fact of it in his face,
terror and the joy of terror,
the pike down there in his soul,
making up its mind without
thinking, moving up and down
like a submarine by shifting
molecules of gas from its blood
to its swim bladder, not a motion
of the body involved, waiting
to clamp fish, frogs, children,
sideways in its teeth, nothing
to do with consciousness,
with will, and here is Zach
to tell me, as if I hadn't been there
myself, watching the worst
come up because I fished it
up out of its waiting, and almost
went down with it, to the green

and gloom, to the churning
ghosts. As if I hadn't won, too,
when the line snapped,
the weight of it lasting forever
in my skinny arms.

Chicory

I worry about the chicory, that tinge of pink
in the blue, its sunset delicacy, even with its tough
stalk. Those ragged, blunt petal-tips.
Like my high school Pep Club skirt, pleats
sharp as knives, but someone could easily get
under it. The road here is crooked, cars fly by
at forty-five or fifty. I worry about how few walkers
there are, how alone nature is, out there
sprouting and budding and dying. Can the utterly
unnoticed survive? What about the farthest
reaches of the universe, the other solar systems?
There's a lot that doesn't seem to need us,
but the negative space around the flower
is what shapes the flower, so the neglect
of such a powerful mind as ours must collapse
its bloom at least a little. So much reciprocity
necessary to exist: we actually exchange DNA
with those we catch diseases from. The germs
travel to our lymph nodes, carrying a bit
of our infector: we become our enemies!
The quality of our existence is that delicate,
which is why I ran from room to room, comforting
my mother, stacking up my father's mess,
wiping my poor brother's drool. No, that's not
right. I was only holding them all in my mind
to keep them from flying apart. How tired I was,
my little body a strung bow. How small
I'd keep things, little flowers by the roadside,
if I could. I would think of them day and night.

VII

FROM *NO NEED OF SYMPATHY* | 2013

Year of the Tent Caterpillars

Tent caterpillars are letting themselves
down their almost invisible threads,
a horror movie of caterpillars, thickly
entwined on the walls and crushed into
a sticky sidewalk mass. They are down
my back, in my hair. I like it, though,
from up close when the sun's behind
and each one's tiny hairs glisten
like a teenage boy's gelled spikes. And
furthermore when I float in my kayak
over the ancient boat sunk beside
the dock and the tires fastened together
like ghostly underwater flowers,
all now encrusted with zebra mussels
(every stick, every chain and tire,
their tiny shells piling up, sucking out
the water's life until it's clear
as the Caribbean), I'm guiltily unsure
if I would change it back again.
As with the caterpillar's glistenings,
one scooch after the other, tiny body
waving along. As with the ones I've loved,
gradually going, those I hardly see
anymore, too, the veil keeps falling away
and I'm left with these worms feeling
for the sky, and whom do I turn to,
to say this is more than I ever thought,
and no worse than what it is?

For

"I'm leaving you," she said, "for you make me sick." But
of course she didn't say that. She *thought* the "for"; she admired
its elegant distance, the way it's wedged like an iron strut
between result and cause, the way it's almost "far," and dire

as a raised eyebrow. She liked the way it sounds like speaking
through a cardboard paper towel tube, using it for a megaphone;
not loud, but strong, all those compacted years shoving
out the other end, as if she were certain she wanted to be alone.

Or

The first four bars of Beethoven's Sixth, the *Pastorale*,
repeat and repeat, always with variation: *or*, and *or*,
something to violate expectations, not fully antiphonal,
only an oar dipped into the measure to make an interior

swirl, pulling the craft slightly to the side, yet ahead,
still: little cupped trails alongside the mark where
the mind turned, questions were asked, and shed,
before moving on, nothing that can't be repaired.

Nor

As a flower sheds petal after petal, as further tests
strip away one after another of the last hopes for a cure,
as a person shakes into the waste bin all her cigarettes
and goes down the street not knowing who she is, the pure

air of saints is achieved by abandonment: Jesus in the garden
alone, cold moon disappearing, Buddha at the morning star,
mind emptied of its snarl of ignorance. Neither to harden
against loss, nor to welcome it. To let it be who you are.

Sugar, Sugar

It was the trees, their amazing xylem and phloem.
It was the paper-thin cambium layer that made both wood and bark.
It was the leaves that took in carbon dioxide, released oxygen,
and sent the sugars down. It was the sugars, for sure, that ran
everything, the result of all that tossing around, that sucking in
rain, that fluttering evaporation. It was my first Pepsi, its sugar-
fizz, and the frozen orange clouds of the Dreamsicle, the slow
caramel centers of the Milky Way, the pure refined sugar
of them, concentrated, lighting up my body, for I was then
growing like a tree, wanting to get somewhere fast. It was my
mother and my father, the parts of me pushing and pulling,
the strain, the gathering into a bud, into the breast-buds,
into the flowering, the sugary colors of my flowering,
the Covergirl Hot Pink lipstick, the henna hair rinse, staining
my fingertips red. It was so far away, so far from the tip
of a tree to the ground, yet the waters traveled through the narrow
tubes and arrived from roots and leaves, and the trunk slowly
thickened with its quiescent heartwood that shored up
all the rest, that was, really, quite finished with all the rest,
that let itself be wrapped by the sugar-hyped layers, so it could
think. It was not really thinking. What was it doing,
not bothering to call itself happy or sad?

The Purpose of Poetry

1

The truth of it is, the stars won't give us any more
answers. We've sailed that way as far as we can.
Anyway, the Chinese discovered everything first.
What did it get them? The emperor Zhu Di
forced six million laborers to build the huge junks,
killing half in the process, most of starvation. The palace
burned; he renounced travel. They buried sixteen
screaming concubines alive with him when he died.
Add that to the horrors we already know, there's a kind of
trance, like watching TV, pixels instead of stars.

2

On *Law and Order*, the boy's father beats the soccer coach
to death because he thwarts his son's chance
for a scholarship. When we run out of oil, no TV.
Notice when the machines go out in a modern house,
it's like living in a corpse. Oil is heavier than poems.
Poems think that when the oil is gone, they'll sing
a ballad of when lights came on with a flick and you
could fly down the road so fast birds couldn't
remember you. Poems think they're on *Restore America*.
They'll scrape the ugly green paint off the fireplace stone
and bring back the superior life of the past.

3

Or they will stuff the terrible suffering into some
decorative urn that will ferment it into Beauty.
But the Big Bang is speeding up. All of this good will
is flying apart, and the poem is getting to be
about as sturdy as a spaceship made out of eyelashes.
It acts more and more like people trying to make love

after too much to drink, the climax always ahead
until the blank moment when it's gone.

4

Or like the birds outside our window. They think
the glass is the whole sky, some of them, but when
they hit, the other sky takes over, the one they never
thought of. I don't know why it's always the house wrens
and the sparrows, the least showy, the ones who live
in the Ninth Ward.[1] Poems keep trying. On TV,
I read the bios beside the pictures of those
killed in Iraq, seven or eight a night,
ranging in age from 19 to 45. I feel
the bios longing to be verses of an epic. In possibly
the oldest epic, Gilgamesh sits with his dead
friend Enkidu, whom he loves like a lover. He "veils
his face like a bride, paces around him like an eagle,
like a lioness whose cubs are trapped in a pit." He tears
his hair out. Why did Enkidu die?

5

Because of a dream. Because he believed he would die.
This is the poem reminding itself how powerful
it is. Where do the dead sit? They sit
in pitch darkness dressed in feathered garments
like birds. What could be more like living? If Enkidu

---

1. It's sad how even the most terrible things turn into footnotes. Students will read
the footnotes before the poems. They will skip the poems.

could open the lid, living would be the very
pupil of his eye, his own TV screen. Captain Kangaroo
is dead, Mr. Green Jeans is dead, Mr. Rogers is dead.
Veterans with their quiet ways put on their old
uniforms and salute the flag, but the poem is pacing
like an eagle, tearing its hair. "Why don't you just say
what you mean?" people say, especially the students.

6

But now the poem's occupied with the most seemingly
trivial tasks, like asking, "Where do the lost
shopping carts go? Where do the angels toss
their garbage?" And since there will be absolutely no room left
in the Cherry Hill landfill after 2012, the poem
is thinking it will clear its throat then and try singing again.

The Kayak and the Eiffel Tower

The white sheet I remember, flashing across
the bed and I was watching my mother and the crying
and the bed disappeared and all was white
but it was not snow, it was my mind, and then, oddly,
she took us in a taxi to the movies, I think
it was *Ben Hur*. It was his postcard, now I know,
from that woman in the Philippines, back when
he was a soldier. All this, a movement
of shapes, nothing to hold onto. The kayak
is like that. It slides through the water and the paddle
goes on one side, then the other, and there is the sway
of the boat and then the correction. It was
like that, and it was like the Eiffel Tower, all filigree
and lace, because I couldn't see anything solid,
but of course it was night and the movie was over,
I guess, but I remember the feel of her body,
her coat against my coat and the sidewalk rough
the way a child remembers the sidewalk: closer
than it will ever be again, grain after grain, and down
inside the grains, the press of earth that made
the grains, and the grinding that broke them apart,
and there were cracks in the sidewalk, and I swayed
a little as if I were in a kayak, not breathing but
sliding through with my mind so far away it was
on a lake, far out, and the shore wasn't the wool coat
my mother wore, not the coat, not anywhere.
And where was my father? Home, maybe, while
all this was rising from the bottom like a log, or a huge
gar, all the way to the top of the Eiffel Tower, while
my kayak dreamed its way off into some other story.

My Father and Hemingway Go Fishing

Both of them would rather fish alone, but Hem asks
about the good spots here in the Antrim Chain,
a few miles from Walloon, so my father gets up
way before dawn, before he is my father, and rows
to the Ellsworth bridge, where Hem is already
fiddling with his canvas pack. My father says get in.
This is the double-oared rowboat, so they both
row, ker-flunk, ker-flunk, oars in the locks in the dark.
They row through Benway, Wilson, the Green River.
Nothing can touch them, no one is up. One war
is over and another has not begun. When the sky
lightens, they can see each other, outline first,
both of them strong-jawed, dark, gorgeous,
but Hemingway does not know he is Hemingway
and my father does not know he is my father.
They scarcely know they are together because it is
the fish they want. It is better to have a third thing.
They are almost at the mouth of Six Mile Lake,
the blips on the surface, quick roiling underneath.
The bank is the cedar swamp with the cedars
slanted across the stream that in the stories are going
to stand for all the banks and all the streams.
The scholars will be climbing around, verifying.
They will say no, not this one. But there is the bottle
of grasshoppers, even dark ones, from a fire.
And their trousers are rolled and wet.
Who is to say that my father was not erased
from this later? Who is to say that they ever wished
to be together eternally? It was never anything
but the fish, the heaviness, the power, not to be

held, then held. Years after, even with me
in the boat, trying to cast my small line out, trying
to get one word of praise, it was the fish. I blame it
on Hemingway, and the cold water that pulled
the heart-blood inward, to steady its own small craft.

Roofers

Five roofers are wedging off the old,
scraping it over the edge. Great black birds
diving in front of the window.
In another place, a nail gun goes off in patterns
of four, sometimes five. They're nice guys:
one has a funny beard that sticks
straight out, one has a lip ring. One is pounding,
testing for rot. One is flipping sections of shingles
down; I hear them slap like clown's feet,
something out of Shakespeare. They know
what they're doing and they do it,
great rolls of thunder, the roof
of heaven cluttered with gods: Homer's
Tityus, Leto, Tantalus, the ones
who work the obscure jobs, who come
when called, the ones before Milton's great-
voiced dignitary, before Hopkins' rod bearer,
the ones from the old days, from my old days,
when over my head, there was music
in the air, the pitch of my church-camp voice,
raised out of the heat and the breeze
and the sun on the spillway rocks, all of it
holding me in as if I were in a shadow-box,
the kind someone looks through
a peephole and everything is 3-D, so the eye
is like the Important God. It fills me
with tenderness, the little world I had going on
inside, my grief that it was not the world.

Hare's Breath

We examine the toilet, hold the ball-cock up,
determine the flapper fails to fully fall.

We put a new one in, snip off the excess chain.
The tank fills only one-third full. We lower

the chain, change the settings on the dial,
flush over and over, studying the maddening

levels until the mechanism settles into
balance as inexplicable as this life we live,

machines coming on and going off, gears
spinning like dreidels on their perfectly honed

tips, a hair's breadth, or hare's breath, or hair's
breath, the metaphor long messed up,

all sense of origin gone, which no doubt explains
why we're floating, wavering, letting gallons

of water pass through, running up the bill.
I ask you, what volume can a hare breathe,

its tiny lungs pumping carroty air? How wide
is a hair? Furthermore, by what tiny margin

did the quarks and leptons have to increase
over anti-quarks and anti-leptons to let matter

win out over anti-matter, to bring us here,
to the flushing of toilets, filling of tanks?

God, God

We dressed for church. I had a white hat
and white gloves when I was fifteen, no joke.
You had to do that to show God you cared.

God's eyes were stained glass, and his voice
was pipe organ. He was immortal, invisible,
while my pantyhose itched and my atheist

father chewed his tongue and threatened to run
out the door but didn't for my mother's sake,
and she swallowed her fate, this marriage,

like a communion cracker, and my brain-
damaged brother lurched around the church
nursery, and my sweeter sister watched me

with huge brown eyes to see what I'd do next.
My God, why did I turn my eyes upward when
we were all there, then, in the flesh? I am so

sorry about *God*, sorry we fastened that word
to the sky. *God*'s not even legal in Hebrew.
If you get the vowel caught between the two

consonants of your lips, it can carry you
dangerously up like a balloon over what you'd
give anything to be in the middle of, now.

Dancing at Your Wedding

I wish I hadn't danced like that, un-
dignified, wild, but consider your groom's
family, full press of uncles, aunts, parents,
generations of sticking together, then your own
scattered mess of faithlessness, and there
you are, father on one arm, me on your other,
two captive animals lured to the same pen.
There I am on the old VCR tape,
flouncing, you could say that,
into the reception with my new man,
your ex-stepfather crazily lurking
in the background. I'm wearing the filmy,
matronly mother-of-the-bride-thing, grief
and joy thrashing in me like Sumo wrestlers.
There we are, all layers of time
licensed to be here, and I am the smoke
of the speed of the rewind, in my smoky
blue dress among the calla lilies
and candles, and you a grand beaded
snowy island, a bell-voice at the microphone,
thanking us all, in general, and then I'm dancing
and dancing, stricken and turning, turning
my eyes. Imagine if Hades followed Persephone
back into spring and summer, not speaking,
sitting at a side table fingering the stem
of his glass, cupping its bowl, smiling
with his white teeth! Imagine if Rousseau
got up to speak of the goodness of the human heart,
and yours still bloody, the sweet smell
of a gardenia loud as a band
playing just under your chin.

Child Labor

Child labor is desperately sought by both the manufacturers
and the starving children. Morality is another one of those words.

Sometimes there's a haze of words, sometimes a fog. My breath
is one of the two. The palm of my hand is a shallow lake,

enough to hold stones and lose words in. The world is held
in God's hand. We sang this on the spillway at church camp

as fingers of water spread out below. True, the earth's crust
miraculously hangs on against the breath of all our talk, our tossed-

around ideas. Factory workers and children still forage in the dumps
at Phnom Penh, and under them, rats and bacteria eat away

at the garbage, and below everything, the earth's core swelters
in its own juices. Isn't it odd that we knew hell was down, heaven

was up, before we knew about the core? I would like to discuss
the consciousness that mumbles to itself so that it won't hear

the hum of sewing machines in the vast rows of warehouses
and the children's pleas for bathroom passes. How consciousness

skips along on the level sidewalk of words as if it were headed
to a picnic. Heraclitus says everything is fire. We have lit a fire

in the barbecue pits, and the thighs of the large people who shop
at Walmart are on fire, but they can't help it. Things got heavy

so fast, to the point of combustion. It was the corporations who
got the children to make the T-shirts, it was the luminous ads

in the *Sunday Times* that sold the shirts, it was the carefully placed
words in the ads, God, we are all jabbering away while hell

cooks the hot dogs and heaven rains the iced sodas, and along
the banquette are the pump dispensers of ketchup and mustard.

Here, in Silence, Are Eight More

Night after night the photos of dead soldiers
go by on the *News Hour* like playing cards while we drink

our wine, though we stop for that length of time, of course,
out of reverence, but it's not enough. The well of

how-not-enough-it-is is bottomless, deeper than TV. Even
if you track back through the Comcast cable, back to

the electrical impulses, you're not even close to what to do.
Not even if you end up on Main Street in Sallisaw, Oklahoma,

and follow the nineteen-year-old into the storefront full of
uniforms, crisp, medallioned, follow not his vanity

but his hope, his longing for order, for the squared shoulders
of order, his wish for the vast plains of the world

to unroll at eye-level, so he can walk out into the particulars,
the screaming, the blood. Owen, Brooke, Sassoon: what

anthem for the doomed youth this time? His death rests
like a quarter in the pocket, a sure thing. Its arrival

is a few missing lines I fill in, wrongly, because
the mind does that: I have him watching in slow motion,

with love and pity, the flowers beginning to bloom
on his shirt, the sky closing like a book. Sadly, then,

he disappears entirely into my mind, his last breath
easing between my words. There was a book in his childhood.

No, mine. Ducks cross the road, a mother duck leads them
through traffic to the pond. The pages flip so that

the ducks seem to move. They slide into the pond
with the satisfaction of making it through the human

confusion. Our soldier floats like a duck. Like a night-flight
casket. In the photo his eyes, straightforward, being all

they can be, float on the surface of a pool of uncataloged
genetic material. One snapshot in time, his eyes were

like that, his mouth. He can't remember. He never was
like that. He was playing dress-up, then, hoping to make it true,

and did, so true no one could get in a word, in protest.

Short History of Music

When I think of the taxi driver,
also I think of London's birds
who only sing at night,
the one silence left to be heard in.

It's the Muslim driver from Pakistan
who steers me two hours through traffic from Gatwick
to St. John's Wood, where the rich Americans live.
His mother's ill, he says; they've brought her to London,
the father remaining. Remaining with his own
upholds him, he says, and I'm fingering
the deep gash in the upholstery; I'm down
to the steel. "We try to forgive,
Madam," he says, "but when Americans
burst down our doors with guns . . . ."

Birds live completely inside their song,
throwing it out at intervals like a plain chant,
clear notes, each a single insistence.
In the night it enters the consciousness
like a dream hidden under bed sheets,
or pressed to the pavement under the heaps
of garbage bags in the street.

A single voice, like the one Palestrina wrote in
to sing the Scripture: all the others
in the background, holding their long notes.

Before him, Pythagoras and his triadic tones
gathering up our Western chords like small armies.
Even though others may call out while we sleep,
all we can say is "Sorry, sorry, sorry."

Big Bang

The whole blessed universe was steam
and density until the crucial moment
came, and blam! a billion billion different
ways to go, one of them this hawk, building up
tension for a dive. As when:

(1) a column of smoke breaks into chaos,
(2) you know you married the wrong man,
(3) in Casablanca, Rick sends Ilsa away,
to save the world.

"We'll always have Paris." Ha. Hold
one pose long enough, birds fly off branches.

The hawk barely shifts.
Somewhere below, a mouse, maybe,
holds perfectly still, feels the change of air.
It loves its life. The hawk loves its life.
The hawk loves the mouse. At the last,
the mouse looks straight into the eye
of doom, is eaten by its doom, becomes
its doom, no doubt is in love with it, now
that it's all doom itself.

It's the bipolar universe, off meds,
where all the excitement is. Ego, superego, id,
out to destroy each other, then growing all mushy
at the final moment when Good seems to have won out

over various Evils, which is an anagram for Elvis.
Elvis, had he lived, might have been like Mick Jagger,
still a bad boy at sixty-three, but singing flat.

Watch him dance on the far edge, headed for
chaos. We're all quivering on a black-hole's edge.
The difference between falling in and not
is one to the fifteenth decimal place, and
it does no good to hold your breath.

Worms

Worms can replace parts.
They can restart themselves
if they're cut apart. And
the slime they leave behind
glues the earth together.
They have no eyes.
Imagine scrunching alone
through life, armless,
legless, and blind
yet so convinced
of your usefulness that it
makes some kind of sense.

Felled Tree

Dear swollen-trunk maple, deemed
diseased by the saw-happy tree guy,
you who have stood silently, supposedly
slipping your ailment through your roots
to the neighboring trees, now fallen
full-blast down, geometrically down,
right-angle, then parallel at last, your flat-
sawn stump blotched with incriminating
evidence—you came and leafed
and are gone, and I who have grown old
in your lifetime, who intuited you rather
than knew you, felt you in my bones,
now feel the slightly thinner woods,
the hint of frailty. Scott the tree guy
has carried your eighteen-inch logs in his
red wheelbarrow and stacked them
for winter: a little Williams, a little Frost.

　　Oh, tree, everywhere I look
I have to pledge reclamation, fill
the forest floor with ferns, mushrooms,
pine needles, and in the side corner
place the outhouse, practically unused
anymore, still in good shape, emitting
its rich human-waste smell, its wood
smell, its few spiders climbing
their trellises with their sticky feet.
Oh tree, so much has been discovered
to fill in the space where you were:
seven new species of Philippine
forest mice, a new genus of blind
Bulgarian beetle, four new species
of jewel beetles, six of New World
micro-moths. I have filled my notecards,

I have left the vertical space open
for the ur-tree, the canonical vision
that will take your place, even the stigmata,
your bulged and arthritic joints, the
whither of your leaving, the grand word
whither standing where you were.

Translation

The woman with the pale hair is signing
the poem. Not that kind of signing.
Her hands dip and flutter and hop
against the black backdrop.
Her mouth shapes emoticons.
Really, I'm not sure what
the mouth's for. I watch her lips,
the poem changed to hieroglyphs.
She makes her eyes turn off and on.
Keats's could do no better. *Still
wouldst thou sing and I have ears in vain.*
Her face goes from happy to pained.
She is inside the poem where the birds live
with their hollow mouths.
I am watching her more than I'm listening.
The poem is not something she believes.
It has sprouted on her like leaves.
It has come out the other side of itself.
Which makes me wonder if I will ever
be able to recover from language enough.
Those people who pray with their palms up
as if they're catching or releasing
electromagnetic waves?
This is definitely not me. I'm following
the words as if they were closed captions
for the trumpets and blazing of the Rapture.

Building a Cathedral

In Barcelona, the massive gothic Sagrada Família sprouts
    its native-species gargoyles—lizards, etc.—according to Gaudí's
plans, an astounding city of stalagmites growing "from nature,"

as he said, even though he died in 1926, twelve years into it, leaving
    a three-dimensional miniature to work from, all based on
the golden ratio: arches like trees, columns like plants, windows

like marine diatoms. Meanwhile, my father has found that if
    he sets the microwave for 1:29, the rotation will stop with
the cup handle facing out so that it can be most easily removed.

Occasionally it takes 1:33, depending on the cup. He has calculated this
    carefully over a period of time, a timeless truth. He's ninety-two
and has nothing but time, wandering around his nice clean retirement

cottage without his tools, his bicycle, his boats. Furthermore,
    he's managed to remove the point of a ballpoint pen cartridge
and tape it to another cartridge so that he can blow the ink from one

to the other when the point of one is stopped up. No waste there.
    He's using up his days organically. I wish I could go back
to Gaudí here, but my father's too compelling. How much longer

will I have him to show me what to do and not to do? His legs
    are getting weak although they retain the residuals of good genes
and a life of motion. He wouldn't call it exercise. He's found an exact

combination of kerosene and oil that keeps his Windsor mantel clock
    running and on time for about a week, after which the kerosene
dries up and the clock slows down again, not that it matters any more

or less than any other human endeavor, not that anything much
    matters to my father anymore, which I notice is a frequent
condition of extreme age and makes me wonder if it isn't perfectly

natural to back out of life slowly, reducing our interest to the diatomic,
 the minute minute. Even his sweetie isn't much to him,
demented as she is, but they sit every evening at his place, TV blaring,

and he puts his hand in hers. They don't seem to be thinking
 of anything, not even the show, just waiting like Vladimir
and Estragon in *Waiting for Godot*. My father makes her lukewarm tea

the way she likes it and nods and says what's necessary to prove
 he's there as she retells the ancient past again. On the phone
he tells me he'd rather be dead if it wouldn't hurt, or hurt

anybody. In the play, Godot doesn't arrive and the hanging-rope breaks,
 and Estragon's trousers fall down, and they do it all over again
the next day. It's an important play. It shows us being us, although

it's not much fun. Beckett is an important playwright. We had to read him
 in school. It was all true, but we were too young to care.
If we were born astride the grave, we were going to swing across

on a Tarzan-rope yelling and beating our chests. We were going to
 build cathedrals and other stuff. Some of us did, some didn't.
This part is almost over for my father. When my Nana lived in Colorado,

where they moved her when Granddaddy died, she made a rooster
 out of seeds in the home's craft class. How stupid to end
your life gluing seeds to a board, I thought, but my mother hung it

on the wall where it stayed long after my mother's own death,
 until my father sold the house. When we threw it
in the dumpster, it felt, cruelly, as if now I could start over, really.

Talk Radio

On the conservative talk radio show he asked me
why I write poems, since no one reads them.

I didn't like the ironic way he looked at me,
as if the two of us shared a dirty secret.

I wouldn't have a secret with him for anything.
I wouldn't tell him about the poems if he tied me up

with an American flag, how the poems and I
look at each other with deeply yearning eyes

as in the old movies that show only a bit
of flesh, a half-second shot

of a finger touching a nipple. How I get excited
at even the thought of a poem,

discouraged when inside it turns out to be
all tensed up, full of itself. How the margins say to me

in their ragged voice, "We could do this
on our lunch hour and no one would be the wiser."

Stashed / fires thrash / and brighten,
flare into blanks. I want to lick those words.

I would follow them up the dark stairs at noon.
I would never tell him how I love even

the frustration, the secret parts where rhyme upends
or comes back with an unfixable rupture, bent

words almost bleeding in their desperation to repent
and satisfy exactly, as God intended.

Fourteen Lines

The young can't understand the concept of time.
They get the way it opens like a flower, but they don't
see when it's reached the edge of itself. They don't realize
when images no longer matter, when the anecdotes that
once seemed everything lurch out front, garish as puppets.
They still believe in profound summations. When you
grow old, you believe in punctuation, in the imposition
of the period, the twin headlights of the colon, the slight
stumble of the semicolon. You look across the floor
littered with nouns and verbs the way a mother
does at the end of the day. Nothing should go on
too long. This is why you sit down and apply the period.
You are not refusing but stopping, which is another thing.

VIII

NEW POEMS

The Swan Flies Straight at Me

My three favorite death paintings: Blake's *Great Red
Dragon and the Beast of the Sea*, a more viciously
potent duo you never saw, and Bacon's *Study after
Velázquez's Portrait of Innocent X*, all vertical slashes
as if Innocent were being lifted into a draft of terrifying
impermanence, and Goya's *Saturn Devouring His Son*,
one of his "black paintings," the ghastly white little body
limp and shining out of the gloom, head already gone.

But what do I know of this vast subject in art, and
for that matter, what did the swan know, who came
huge, sudden as if straight at me, muscular wingtips
skimming the water until it was even with me a few
feet out, stretched out, mad with concentration,
prying the sky apart as it passed, what did either of us
know of our end except what we make of it in our
separate minds that cry into the gloaming we long

to outrun, or paint safely down? Or gather up a word
or two to cover the situation, this is what I do, *happily*
do, by the way, which is why I recall with such *frisson*
turning on the dock, coming face-to-face with the subject
bearing down, and why I stood right there on the end
with my glass of wine, and the kind of unconscious smile
I imagine a hunter might get at the movement of leaves.

Elegance

    I thought I had hold of something elegant, a luminescent glow
on the lake, a flicker's flash of headdress high on the tree.

I thought I heard a conversation from over water, someone saying
laissez-faire, or *Toulouse-Lautrec,* but it was only guys fishing,
a mishearing that came to me like a ray of light through stained glass,
a shimmer like a fine line of Milton's, or a landscape by Monet,
applied in layers.
    What I wanted was something privately
apprehended, something slowly and privately understood:
elite, yes, I admit it.

A pontoon boat came by. I would rather be on one of those,
studying the accommodating landscape as if it were a museum,
    than on water skis, for example,
terrifyingly public and sudden, which is why I'm fond of

the Turneresque, or of an aspen leaf, half-unhinged over and over,
a sibilance of rhythm that works the atmosphere the way
Noah wavers the sailboat rudder back and forth to inch toward
the gust.
    I don't know the name for this maneuver.
And when the wind completely stops, there's the small slurp
against the side of the boat that's exactly what I mean,
    the delicacy of the mundane, observed
and properly incorporated in service to the whole.

Another example at present: the gull has adroitly
caught in its beak the tiny bass Noah just tossed back
and is carrying it flapping, sunward.

Unfurl

Two point six minutes on video: roses,
irises, daffodils, lilies, mums, opening
and opening as if opening
were the meaning of life, hard
to believe at my age. I watch for
the slightest caving of petals
at the edge of editing, before
the next opening, the hidden
collapse, the withering, but
it's only the poetry of opening.
    Prose goes on almost
invisibly, but when the lines
begin to shrink, the teachers want
to return and dig them up one
by one the way Emerson dug up
his wife's coffin, unwilling to have
the end be the end, following
the relentless trail from bloom
to, well, the unspeakable, and
onward, if that's the word for
what's directionless and simply
what is, even the words for it
cluttering the sight, even the sight
cluttering sight. Might as well
exhume Cleopatra, who, contrary
to popular opinion, almost certainly
used a nice, soothing poison, not
an asp, in the tale that continues
to rise out of the dead ends
of her own self, transmogrified
into Elizabeth Taylor's version of

Shakespeare's version: unrolled
in gold from a carpet, as gorgeous
in death as a blossom opening,
arms falling against the floor like
petals spread, sexy and done-for.

The Undoing

He bought the house to burn it down.
He bought the land to burn down the house.
He loved a thing for its demise, its sundering,
for birds flying through as if the house were a removed window.
The walls were still sturdy, there was furniture,
which he allowed friends to carry off. He bought the flames,
the crumbling, the pitch, the roof bowing and giving.
Give has that meaning as well.

And now the outhouse that belongs to the Muellers
has given way, opened like a flower in the woods near us.
The house itself is dark-faced, incomprehensible, what's left.
Where are the Muellers? Don't tell me you don't feel
those losses, too, that you wish you'd seen the burning,
the outhouse burst open, that you aren't tantalized.

At the top of Woody Knoll hill the ancient Airstream
is on its side. I wish my childhood would precisely
reconstruct itself so I could see what it was I didn't see,
vulgar or not. I wish I could burn it down, but it is already
burned to the ground. He watched the house burn.
The firetruck came and watched it burn. It was *his*
burning, he tended it with his eyes since it was barely
contained, spit and whistle and swirl, hunger
and satiation swallowing each other. It feels wrong.
The old wasn't that bad. It just kept on being a threshold.
It kept on undoing itself so the burden could shift.

News

Maybe the sperm lugged it along from the dim past
when it crashed into the egg. What had gone wrong,
what switch switched at the least opportune moment?
What moment in my childhood was the final, unbearable
one? Which breeze blowing the sprayer chemicals back
in my face? I kept on living forever until it was too late
for that. Last night we left the window open
and Wally the cat spent the night, apparently, watching
what he wanted but could never have.
We with our big bodies hugged the bed, sleeping
through the news we wanted to refuse, anyway.
Wouldn't we have murdered in our minds
the Syrian government troops, wouldn't we have yelled
at the kids who painted graffiti on the bridge?
But Wally said why howl at the moths on the screen?
Why not just remain wakeful to the inscrutableness
of spring's open window? He didn't really say this.
The overhead fan was turning and I couldn't hear
what he said. My mind was on a little train.
I was eating my lunch on the train, spilling onions
from my sandwich. I had a banana, too. No, a big yellow
bus I mistook for a banana. And the onions,
something not quite right, oh yes, it was the world
coming back to me. The school bus rumbling
on our brick street, full of kids who don't yet know
how long the past will last as their bodies grow.

On a Day That Bombs

On a day that bombs were being dropped by drone aircraft
in several regions of Libya, blowing apart fragile bodies,
many of whom were living their sincere and momentary lives,
it was a perfect day here except for the wind and the flies.
The flies were too large to ignore. It was 73 degrees.
The woods smelled of pine, and there were squirrels and
chipmunks. A thousand mayflies that had died overnight
waved at me from the porch. I could hardly be present
for both, could I?—the bombs and the mayflies. So I chose
one, then the other, like closing one eye, then the other,
watching the subtle shift from one side of the nose
to the other, or you could shift a chair from one side
of the table to the other and make a whole different room.
Both sides' urgent consequence. I think of the word
fragile: its dual syllables a form of concealment,
both history and mystery, sun and shade. I don't know
what is appropriate in this world. The Jews mix bitter herbs
with the Passover meal for the bitter lives of the slaves
in Egypt. It strikes me how sane the Jews are,
after all their abuse, their homelessness, and how intensely
insane. I think of Philip Roth, Isaac Singer, Yehuda Amichai.
Why do I always think of an irrational violin in a minor
chord, not human, not even a bird-cry, more like the sound
of neutrinos slipping through everything, grazing the edges
as they pass, just a small scratch, but adding up.

Feeding the Maggots

Every day this week Abby has joyfully reminded me,
"It's time to feed the maggots!" I unfasten
the elastic strap that keeps the raccoon out,
pop up the plastic lid, and there they are, chewing
away, little rice-size devourers, caressing the mush
of cake, banana skins, bones, bread, apple cores.
She loves the shiver of what's going on down there,
the eating and birthing in the dark of what we've left
behind. I don't like to empty the garbage, myself,
don't much like to pull away the cover over the causes,
the suffering, the tombs, the pyramids, the forest roots.
What happens when it freezes, this far north?
Have they all turned to flies by then? Is life a rehearsal
for death? Then why this satisfied squirming? Why
will the bones go, too? Why was my dollar bleached
in the wash? Those love poems of the human animal
with all their angst and fear and irony and ennui
and dirty talk, they are so excited! And look! The raccoon
has dug down on either side and up from the bottom.

Bees

Here come the bees,
the innumerable bees,
their small brains on fire
for the peanut butter and honey
of my youth, carried all morning
deep into the pathless woods
behind the cottage.
Sweat bees, dark and scant
of body—their sound *scant*,
scant. Why did I love so
to be afraid? If they sting me
now I will be glad of it,
of their sharpness, their crisp
shells, their fairy wings.

I will be glad for their partisanship,
their swarming like the waft
of a hand that knows what's best,
their conductor's grand gesture.
I will be glad even for their sticking
in thick honey, twisting
with a quiet, intimate fatality.

They have come back from
far away because I was too young
then. They move into all this
absence, into the subdivisions
named glade and hill and wood.
They are the ones who know how
to pierce the space around
my one-and-only sandwich with
their personal, pointed grief.

Taxol

I was just thinking about the paradox of the word chemotherapy—that it's healing/curing: therapy, a word whose root has very much to do with care also—ministering; in the Iliad and Odyssey even a squire could be called a Therapon—the one who administered to the hero, putting on and taking off his armor, etc. . . .

And chemo is chemistry, potentially substances that aren't normally encountered in the body . . . But you know what? I thought a little further in my nerdy little etymological brain, and I believe the chem part, taken from alchemy, is originally the Egyptian [khem], which is the precious fertile earth from the Nile flood, the black gold from which alchemists tried to derive the metal gold.

So, that may be something. "Ministering to the body with precious black-gold earth?"

MY STUDENT ELA

The molecule that oddly binds to a cell's
hollow tubes, that holds them in paralysis, that stops
    their wild replication.

That requires all the bark from one rare yew
in the old-growth forests of the Pacific Northwest to save
    one person. Also the home

of the rare northern spotted owl.
Now you're up against the press of need, of cost.
    The bloody essence, the drug-war

of it. Everyone's stake. Don't sleep under the yew
if you don't want bad dreams. In ancient English graveyards,
    where the yew's planted

over graves, rats die. Let the roots
talk to the dead, as the Druids did. There was the woman
　　who only touched

the hem of Jesus's robe and was cured.
Likewise, it turns out that simple needle-cells grown
　　in fermentation tanks,

a brew, an essence, is enough. But will this
life be saved? Won't it? I ask this with reverent earnestness,
　　as the complicated foreignness

enters my small vein, chilly as a stream
through underbrush: Taxol, making a pressure, an ache
　　farther down my arm,

where the nurse places a warm pack
to loosen the valves, the barriers, to keep death's molecules
　　going where they're meant,

into the deep forest of the body,
mine, mine, only one of me in existence. Who touched me?
　　Jesus asked, so subtle the solution.

Cancer Support Group with Painting by Monet

The door swings from cold to cold: the institutional
lobby, like a train station, where we meet: a Dickensian
tableau of collateral damage,

except for me, but, I say, "Next week I'll look
like you," to the woman with the hairless baby-look,
blue knit cap loosely pulled, past embarrassment.

She's depressed, in her second round, says her husband,
after being cured for two years. I examine my life
to see what part of it is made of this: I want to fit in.

One cause after the other: train tracks.
We were in Chicago, my sister and I, age nine and twelve, sent
alone (no parent would do that now) to the lake,

by train. The hollow bathroom, the scrub lady,
the old man. I made my sister sit on the bench, not stir.
I meanwhile remained alert, my spine learning control.

The man who came in with me has multiple myeloma.
His pale preoccupation with the body's
failing. What is this love of living that turns to each

failing part, in wonder, in curiosity, as if
it were alien? The conductor waves the train on, after
a brief stop. This time we are on it.

The woman cannot walk without help. It's the neuropathy.
To reach for meaning is to miss everything.
To reach is to miss everything.

Monet made the train bear down through the snow
with persistent hooded headlights and roiling
black smoke. He made the man alongside walk

the opposite direction. Neither has much to do with
the other, yet each appears to be the other's
consequence. The wooden fence and the young trees

are the spine of that dark beauty, holding each other up
by repetition until the end, which is not in the painting.

Snoring

What is that sound
like the memory of a foghorn?
Was that you, snoring, here
in this roomful of others tethered
in their recliners by transparent tubes
dripping chemicals? What quiet suffering
have you intruded upon, what fragile,
joyful thought have you disrupted?

You keep saying "you" because
even the you you know is some distance
from what must be a truer you, the one
others know, maybe, or the one
in the mirror, reversed—you'll never
know her. Or the one faltering
across the room now, dragging her
pedestal stand, headed for the bathroom
with her swinging bags and tubes.

The others are watching. You want do
even this faltering gracefully—
a little beauty where it can be had.
What does anyone want but a beautiful
world? Even the Boston Bombers,
what did they want but some kind
of beauty they could understand?
And then the young one, hiding bleeding
in the boat. Did he think how he might
make his exit worthy of the end
of the world? Did the officer lifting him
gently out, half-dead, know how much
the two of them resembled the Pietà?
No, it was you who thought that,

seeing how valuable the load, so once
beautiful, so fraught with anguish,
so unaware at that moment
of the clamor he caused
around him, its long echo.

Lesson

Atossa the Persian queen, 440 BC, likely had stage 3
    breast cancer. She had a slave take a knife to it.
        I picture this. People have tried

to amputate their own stomachs. No limit to what's been
    cut out to save ourselves. Huge excisions, back then,
        through muscle, ribs, shoulder.

But how can we rid ourselves of ourselves, what's built into
    the genomes—adapting, recovering, repairing,
        desperately, inventively, fiercely—

showing us survival tricks too late, ha-ha, to use?
    Cockroaches are going to crawl over the surface
        of the scorched earth, learning

what's poison, what's not, in four generations. One
    errant cell in the body and you have the Big Bang,
        one bite of one apple,

so to speak, dispersing galaxies. Everything's been tried:
    alcohol, opium, paste of crab's eyes,
        goat's dung, frogs, crows' feet,

tortoise liver, laying on of hands, compressing the tumor
    with lead plates, bleeding, purging, X-rays,
        ghastly chemicals. Sometimes

there's spontaneous remission. Let's say I believe
    in angels, then three years later, there it might be
        again, bulbous, bloated, in charge.

Let's say it's gone forever. This is the lesson. The sky
    can open up for no reason I can see. Stars
        can stay in the heavens

as if this were the plan all along: to flicker
    over and over, a tableau that seems personal,
        full of love, of romance, even.

Mute Swan

1

I am full of irritation this morning
which makes folding the fitted sheet
a disaster, wrinkles smashed inside.
Down at the dock, the swan hissed
at me and I thought, good for you,
swan, what business do we have
in your life, anyway, making up myths
in which you rape or die?
Beautiful things often hiss if you get
too close. Or if you try to neaten them up
like clothes. A swan's neck is tough
enough to twist you into knots.
Beauty, I don't know how to feed it
without getting bitten.

2

Swan's wings are heavy enough to kill you.
Eleven swans at once have traveled our lake
in perfect synchrony in the boat wakes,
their heads so far from the wild bucking,
they seem to have forgotten their bodies.
Terrible flowerings, they are going
somewhere else, to do what they do.

3

A male swan is a *cob*, the female a *pen*.
Who thought those up? They make a kind
of sense, though, the same kind of sense
that turns a swan's neck plus its reflection
into an ice-hook.

4

If a challenger comes too near the nest
the cob climbs on him and shoves
his head down until he drowns. Not shoves.
He rests his beak quietly, relentlessly,
on the neck as if it were the challenger's
decision to bow under and he were
helping him stay there. His big body
covers the other, except for one wingtip.
There's a leisurely quality, like love.

When swans mate, their heads and necks
form a perfect valentine. Or they intertwine
necks. Last night I wanted to watch
the movie unencumbered by your hand
on my breast. I was touchy. You were all
winding; I, all hiss.

Tulips

I am in costume, gamine in my jaunty
blue cap as I loiter outside the saloon.
I crush my cigarette on the sidewalk,
smile with my chipped
but somehow charming teeth.
I am in this movie because I have taken
wig number one to be washed.
Because I am sitting
in my garden, actually, wearing my other
that's nothing but a fringe of hair,
made to seem like hair
under the blue cap. Under the jauntiness
is my secret. I am a tonsured monk,
all day nothing but prayers. It's May.
The street department is filling the awful
deep potholes with black patches,
overlapping the old gray ones. But here
are my tulips, spotlights
on the situation.

Gamin, gamine, I like the feminine,
its bemused curl at the end. I like this cap.
I like my movie, as movie,
in toto, but it seems to have come from
behind, somewhere, and I only have
these two small eyeholes
in the front of my head. I also don't
know how it will end, with its trucks
and patches and the title of the whole
thing I call tulips, even though
they only turn on their red silk
with the sun.

The Elk Farm

Sometimes they're gathered, racks above
the fence line, sometimes far back

on the hill, feeding or dozing or watching
the air's silence, unbroken by you or

your idling car. Sometimes you get out,
tell the kids to look, elk, here. Like deer,

only fed, fatter. Dutifully, the kids stand,
waiting for action. You hope the old

life, the spiked rages, bull roars,
the violence we come from, is at least

intimated by these astonishing, branching
growths, but the small herd wanders

off, the kids hang on the fence for fun,
beg for ice cream, and you, being now

among the docile, after, Lord, those
unspeakable years, say yes, okay, yes,

let us be happy, let the apocalypse come,
let the last moments be of ice cream

with multicolored sprinkles, let the elk
wake up with their hooves, lower their

velvet trees and bugle for all they're worth,
a regular Disney movie, nobody gets hurt.

Edward Hopper's *Automat*

The Automat serves the original and loneliest fast food.
Drop in a coin. There could be no one else in the world,
just you and something made somewhere else.
The young woman sits at the round table,
rows of reflections of lights seeming neither inside
nor out, in the huge black beyond of the window.
The door and the radiator stand to the left, neither
managing to convince the other of warmth or escape.
Her green coat laps open, half between arriving
and leaving. Holding her cup suspended
with her bare hand, the other gloved, she is neither
drinking nor not drinking. Yet on her head is the most
yellow and chic cloche, round and drooping.
It's awkward, this leftover hope, shading the downcast
eyes. Yet, if you approach her, tell her it will be all right—
maybe nothing is wrong. Or maybe what's wrong
is the best thing, her possession, what can't be bought
at the Automat. Maybe she's gone too far to want
to be distracted now, maybe she can see from here
the internal workings, where all is sorted and rearranged.

Silence

The poetic kind, fastened inside Greek light
and summer and birds brought to someone's
attention. The kind that's fastened
inside an avocado, so buttery it's hard to know
you've eaten it unless you use lemon
or salt. The feathery kind inside snow,
that doesn't exist until you shovel it.
Note: silence can't wake up without you.
Specific cells, having gotten lost in a fervor
of their own, God help me, rallied silently into
the garrisons of the lymph nodes. It was early
November, yes, that was the phone call.

Another kind of silence happens when the baldness
shows under the cap. As if the biggest thing
in the universe has been found. Oh! It really has!
So big scientists say it shouldn't exist. Clusters
of quasars four billion light-years across. Each
pure energy surrounding a huge galaxy
with a super-massive black hole at its center.
Nearly everything is a surprise at first,
and unknown at the core. Needles, tests. Then just
what it is: silence opening its dark eye, pointing.

What Happens

You're moving toward or away from,
sailboat rocking softly, no wind,
sails luffing. The dinner bell too far away
to hear, too far to let them know
you don't know how long.
You have so much to say, still,
but of course they'll learn it themselves.
Let sorrow sit down at the table,
let that good meal be mixed with tears.
What are they crying for?
They have words for it, and they use them.
More poetry. This is what happens
and has nothing to do with you.

Fawn

A fawn the size of a cat with long legs was left
in the tall grass in her yard. Mothers do that
until the fawns can keep up—they come back
and get them in early evening. M— knew it was there
because it stood up once. So sweet!
She waited all evening for the mother to come,
the reunion, the way they nuzzle and the baby nurses.
Around 9:30 a doe came and left. Then two more
came and sniffed. The fawn has no smell.
Usually it stands and they spot each other.
It got dark and then cold, cold rain,
even lightning. M— was in agony, truly.
She lived so far out of town, each event was hers,
only. How was the fawn to survive
without the mother's warmth?
She felt she was in charge of life,
        no, it was the weight
of watching, the inability to look away.
It was her country that had abandoned its delicate
balance, the armored tanks, the night-vision
goggles. Nothing but window-glass between her
and foreclosing darkness. Should she try
to warm the fawn in her studio?
What if the mother came? All night she lay,
worrying. She almost got up several times, as if
stirring and pacing would solve this.
At 6:30 a.m. she went out. The fawn was gone.
Mother? Coyotes? Then she saw
the mother's hoofprints with the tiniest hoof-
prints beside. For a moment she felt
shallow rooted, with nothing, nothing in sight,
to show her how to withstand
such violent alternations, such grace.

Wheel

Rain at last. Day sinking like a ship
    into the boom and patter.
Daisies, daylilies, spattered

and dripping, cars plowing a scrim
    of water. I'm grateful the sky's
coming around, a predictable hymn

of cycles. Like the moon and stars
    moored to the end
of our dock, circling my eyes. In Vegas,

the old women in gold sandals
    twirl the bars of cherries,
grapes, bananas. What later do they

say was predictable—
    loss or gain? What prescience
claim? The radiation arm moves

back and forth over me. Past that,
    stars on the ceiling,
what will come out when rain ends,

someone's idea of peace. I'm lying
    low, it's raining out. Periods
are tattooed on my stomach, I've been

mapped for return and return
    with such patient concern.

The War

I am pulling this out of a hat. I want to think I know
my past. The war, my father coming up the walk
in his uniform. A memory made of what I was told?
Before that, the house heavy with women—Nana,
Great-Aunt Rhoda, Mother, Gussie the maid.
Granddaddy's purple heart from WWI framed
on the bedroom wall. What they held of the past
barely touched me. The mixing of yellow into the oleo,
ration coupons. Keep in mind how little I knew
of circumstances, how much I built later. How even
Great-Aunt Rhoda lying in the darkened room upstairs,
the smells and the nurse doing some sort of
cleaning of her wound, may be imagined
to a large degree, what came from a tone,
a darkness, a partially open door. What I guessed
of grief, my mother's tears when the vacuum cleaner
salesman left, her longing, my father's refusal.
The time my mother came back from a neighbor's
house with a pack of Luckies and lit one. My father's
mocking rage, or a general sense of rage, the tablecloth
pulled out from under our lives on any day.
Who knows whether it was, or whether my anxiety
was misplaced and it's me, hearing myself cry from
here for some little girl who never existed, some
accumulated gratitude or shame I have to go to,
to find out who I think I am, what I've amounted to.

Pike

Two of them standing in the water, one on the dock
with the three big flopping pike. Zach is holding
and tilting the laptop. They're watching how to
take the Y-bone structure out. They've asked me
for a sharpener and now Noah's bent over the fish
with the knife and the video going. He's slicing
slowly at just the right angle to catch the bones
and leave no strays. They're all steady and dedicated.
I like watching them. I'm hopeful when I do, because
of the smoothness of their movements, eye from screen
to fish, fish to screen as if the man filleting on screen
is right there on the dock. I am the one still divided
into segments, who hasn't yet learned how distance
isn't distance, only a different medium.
Then for the frying they're doing it again, propping
the laptop on the counter of the tiny kitchen,
flour everywhere, with egg white whipped to a froth,
each piece dipped in that, then into a mixture of—
is that curry, for heaven's sake? Then the intense
collaboration of skillet and hands and screen,
such serious responsibility for it all, for the whole
process, from the clever underwater video they made
themselves, to table, none of the self-consciousness
that sets things apart from each other. They're proud
of getting the Y-bones out. Inside one fish
was a whole lure, wicked big, as big as the stomach,
with its hook, the fish still living until then, still
thrashing until they cut it open and relieved it
of its terrible, deathly burden, everything
turning out exactly as it should.

Muskrat

The muskrat has eaten every one of the water reeds.
I've seen him only once, slipping under the dock.
The summer clouds were shifting. I went inside, then,
to lay my eyes on my possessions. My things,
I knew their names. I don't know the muskrat's name,
yet he was nibbling around the edges of my life,
pulling threads into his den, working his jaws. He may
be a she. She may be making more muskrats. She may
be making so many burrows that the shore will crumble
into the lake. I have been steadfast, haven't I? Yet
there is this loss. I had a dream that I was trying to get
the children to school. It was late. I was on my bike
and Kelly was on roller skates, holding on behind.
We coasted so fast we ended up in New York City.
Then we were really lost. We entered an Iranian embassy.
When I woke up, there was still this residual
responsibility, this weight. What can I say? The muskrat
has her song I can't hear. Or, I'm indifferent to it
in the way siblings at the dinner table just eat, or kick
each other under the table. A muskrat goes by,
edges along the water with her yearning, and later
appears in the mind, a slippage with a tail.
Think about it. And the water was singing in that voice
it has when it wishes to disguise itself as sloshing,
when you have to listen through the sloshing for how
the singing breaks against the rocks.

Tiny Fish

The children fish off the dock
where the minnow-sized ones hover
oblivious to the hook jutting
from the badly threaded worm.
The water's clear enough to watch
victims gather at the bait.
One after the other, hauled in,
tallied up, tossed back.
When the hook goes deep
into the throat, they give
the tiny fish to me, the one who,
on a whim, watched last night
a video of bodies flying
from the Towers over and over,
the camera following down
then returning to the top
to gather up another. There
it was, a YouTube next to
the one I'd meant.

Gently, now, I slide my palm
along the dorsal fin, gently
take the hook in hand
and twist in the open mouth,
oh mercy, the grating squish
of fish transformed
to flesh, which I hold
long enough, twitching its
blessed last, for my hands
to understand one more time
the fix we're in, how utterly
they're attached to me.

Every Day I Touch Things

Autumn came before I realized.
   Sharpness flew up like gull cries,
the swan turned upside down

in the water, pulling up grass,
   rolling its big hips upward,
which made me wonder

if words are necessary for pleasure, if
   without them, sparkles on the water
would be useless baubles.

I have so many of them, touching
   would feel like a wound without
them. When they lag behind,

where have they been? The nuns
   are sure that inside the glass case
is a piece of the Cross. They've hung

that word around its neck.
   Over many years, *wood* and *word*
have caught up with each other.

Even the fierce knot of fibers
   might be glad to hear, before
it's undone, the story it held together.

View from Space

A dolphin, we guessed. We watched a long
time, from the great heights of the cliffs
of Mohr, but nothing rose out of the bank
and slosh. A rock, a disappointment in a scene
we wished magical, alive, back when the two
of us were new, looking for signs. Just that,
though, a scene to join the others, flattened
into the past, the way they all go, even
this year of life-and-death exigency.
What seemed a space cut out of time,
we watch fill with detritus, as it does.

 I'm tired, too tired to drive, you
steer us along the bay, point out rocks almost
submerged. Rocks, not gulls, or one gull
stationed on a rock. Deeper out the water
turns indigo, a guide to where enormities
hide, the sunk ships, the fissures, what did
we want to find, before the bright net of day,
the existing things, kept entering, and we kept
dutifully picking them up on shore, to show
each other: look, this, and this, and what
in the world shall we do with this?

The Gospel Truth

The Confederate soldiers came for the freed slaves.
They had not thought to escape but had been freed
by the Union army. They were being paid wages.
But the Confederate soldiers ripped them from their children,
cut off their hands, branded their faces, dragged them
in groups until they collapsed. Nothing that hadn't been
done before, that isn't done now—one hundred four
people killed this summer in Milwaukee, a hundred twenty
in New Orleans. "More dangerous to be caught without
your gun than to be caught with it," says the police chief.
A ten-year-old child, a "cub of the Caliphate," has beheaded
a Syrian officer. Twenty-five child executioners stand
with their guns pointed at each bowed head in Palmyra.
Before Palmyra itself was rubble. I want to say all this
before I tell you the lake is smooth this morning,
with a faint sheen, the way it is in autumn. That I am not
able to go on with the horror. That it is all true. That poetry
is as awful as the rest, with its face directly in the passing
beauty, with its mourning, its helpless words. How long
it has stood, with its cocked gun, trying to save the world,
to wake it up to the dangers? Its heart has been breaking
for centuries, breaking and raging. It wants to tie you
to the altar, and if God didn't utter the words of release,
it would shed your blood to prove how full of faith it is.
How sure, sure it is, of something yet to be revealed.

Speed

Time has speeded up so much, songbirds
fall behind. Where is Snuffy Smith, and Nina
Gabaldin? Our whole seventh grade class?
They have been resurrected on Facebook;
they email with long autobiographies.
This moving away and return is too frantic
for my mind. It knows it can't see
what's coming so it wants plenty of time
to prepare. My body wants this red fleece
shirt to last forever. It calls that prayer.
My dear one's body keeps making little flowers
of cells the doctor cuts away before they
turn nasty. Many bodies in old age go crazy
like this. Plus, too many people work
too hard and pick up McDonald's hamburgers
on the way home. Their health is wrecked.
Others have no jobs, yet their alarm clocks
still go off in the morning. This is a worse
kind of speed, seen from a standstill.

The quiet moon is still slipping in and out
of its translucent dress, but secretly
backing away inches at a time, so we don't
notice. It is dreaming of flying out of orbit.
Maybe I will witness this after I have come
through the fear and emerged into the whole
thing. Maybe what I thought was speed
will turn out to have been my own mind,
clumsily trying to funnel everything through
one narrow channel. If so, it is wearing me out,
inventing the word *speed* over and over.

Blueweed

Along the road, delicate blue
    trumpets with pink buds
        and hairy, flaring stamen.

Tiny nettles on the stem, because
    the blueweed doesn't want me,
        it wants the bee, wants it

the way the wind wants to move.
    I saw a sign, PRIMITIVE
        YOUTH CAMP, and I was

wading through culverts, poking
    the matted fur of dead cats
        caught in the brush. Primitive

youth: my first cigarette
    at Girl Scout camp, its jolt
        of nicotine, the alternate

world I hadn't known of. I lay
    in the tent, something roiling
        and pitching, besides my

stomach, something dislodged deep
    in the spirit world, something like
        a bee: nearsighted, but

picking up ultraviolet. When I knew
    I was not my body, but that we'd go on
        wanting each other forever.

Refrigerator

I have returned to the refrigerator of my youth,
the one that droops
its shoulders. A small thing,
just noticed, humming in the corner
of my mind. It wears its white lab coat
and shuts at the end of each meal
with a definitive snap, unlike the casual
sighings of the new ones. The old one remembers
the ice pick, the tongs,
it knows its mortality, its vulnerability
to the electrical cord.
It has nothing in its door but door.

It lives in the place rooted in dream
that will not change.
I have returned to my brother after a long time,
because of the refrigerator
that held his medicines, his juice, on wire racks.
I have not told my chiropractor
why my spine is rigid with history,
It is rigid with my brother's spine,
seizing, arms thrown forward, trembling.
My spine knows not when or where
this might occur
again. It is an animal exposed,
a fish eaten down to its Christmas tree.
It is 1955 at my grandmother's
nervous house, with the bubble lights
and the refrigerator in the pantry
and the men's bourbon there,
and my brother hushed up so no one will
worry. History has hold of the situation
and will not alter a bit of it; I see myself

in heroic terms, separated
from myself by the gulf of regret,
the refrigerator keeping its small light
to spill into the darkness
at intervals.

Poem for Record Players

For their relentlessness, their
clever launching of the needle's
secrets skyward, their luring
the needle to the hiccupping
end, for the red record player
by the low beveled window
with hollyhocks outside and
Rusty in Orchestraville turning
and Markie drooling and reaching
his hand to stop the turning, then
drawing it back, remembering.
For Markie with his scratched brain,
his flinging seizures, who would
bump the needle and jump from
the part of "The Swan," by Saint-Saëns,
to the talking oboe, Markie
dancing, the needle floating
hardily along its new groove.

And for the gray living room player,
for my father's Tchaikovsky
and Beethoven, my mother's
Oklahoma and *South Pacific*. For
my silly nostalgia, all of it, even then.
My hopeless longing: the absence
necessary for harmony to enter,
the needle of disharmony to press
against it. "Oh What a Beautiful
Morning," my father is singing,
and my mother is singing in fragile
harmony with the one phonograph

speaker, all poured directly into
the palpitating rooms of my heart.
This is it, Oh, no such bright
golden haze on the meadow, no such
corn high as an elephant's eye.

The Sex Life of Anacondas

We are sitting by my dying mother's bed. My father
is reading aloud from *National Geographic*,
"The Sex Life of Anacondas." He describes the males
wadded around one female into a breeding ball
that can last four weeks. Who knows how
she lives with it? Happily, she is much larger
than the males. They know by her heft which one
she is. My mother is in a coma and likely
cannot hear about the anacondas, although hearing
is the last to go. She has had all of that she can stand,
already. The one lamp is just enough for the magazine.
I get up and lean over her twilit bed. I smooth
her hair, which has almost no gray. I think how
gray is an absence, whereas brown is still fair game.
I lean into her face and shout, "I love you,"
the way the nurses said to do. They say
to her, "I'm going to aspirate your throat now,
Mrs. Brown, so you can breathe better," even though
she keeps on with her soft gasping. Our minds
keep piling on the same old facts, same
old guesswork. Sometimes a spark of recognition
can come at the end. I would like that: some
gathering up of loose threads, some compensation.
In the funeral car,
my father describes how a rotary brake works,
using his middle finger to point as he has for years
since his forefinger tendon was severed by a broken dish—
the gesture with its tinge of sexuality, its up-yours,
that he at other times slyly acknowledges. Our driver
looks straight ahead. To speak of love is hard
here, the way it's hidden in the mechanism
as if one word's as good as the other.

The Bar Mitzvah

The row of goyim, that's us,
family of half the family,
those who don't talk of Israel at dinner,
here because of fate,
because of the strangeness of our children,
because of this grandchild in his tallit,
his kippah, words we read the leaflet to know.
We watch the Torah lifted from its rainbow
tomb, moved that the world's been organized
this other way, too, into this pageant
we both agree and don't agree
is true. Zach pronounces perfectly,
as far as we can tell. Who is this child
who speaks his sermon on the poor,
the ignored?
    It's as if we've crawled into a flower,
petal after petal to the seed,
past its successive cell divisions
to a beginning we can barely imagine.
Imagine, we're all dreaming of being good!
We're dressed-up blooms in a row, rising
and sitting, wearing the little bowls of yarmulkes,
or the women's pinned-on flutter of lace.
And what's the imagination doing now,
tossing on the tallit like Superman's cape?
Did the world begin with form
or formlessness? Which is happier?
Now Zach's carrying the Torah,
warrior triumphant, people kissing its sash.

We're smiling. The Jewish heartbreak
we can never enter, but this child
is beautiful enough to break our hearts:
the distance, the cost, the wild shifts
of language it's taken to get here.

Mummy Exhibit

Jake says it's one turtle on the next one's back,
all the way down. Near bottom are the skulls

wrapped and half-wrapped, turned to stone,
ribs turned up like ship ribs. Grins that say

friends forever, whether you like it or not.
Babies' large heads flattened from eons of rest.

The long bodies of adults, leather on bone,
eyes empty, the bald truth picked out, scanned,

carbon-dated. Jake likes the one in the sarcophagus—
well, not in, but suspended on glass between

its carved halves, a Russian nesting doll ready
to fit. It's a fine afternoon, all of us spinning

on the planet, Jake growing, me crumbling,
moving among mummies held between then

and now. You can almost touch bottom, you stand
rapt for something more, something inside

the inside that surely must correspond to
what's too far up to see, but thank God is holding

very still and has not toppled everything, yet.

Caterpillars

Caterpillars voraciously eat leaves. The ones that look
like leaves themselves eat in a careful pattern
so there will be no rough evidence. They snip off
half-eaten leaves, so the birds can hardly tell
they're there. The hairy, the spiny, the poisonous
caterpillars bluster along, leaving a mess.
Tattered leaves everywhere. The birds know
the difference, which ones to eat. I hid in the culvert
when he chloroformed the kittens in a cooking pot.
He should have had the cat spayed, but it cost money.
Now I can see how he was. Then I only saw the kittens
and then not, buried in the yard. There were many
ways I could hide. I could chew the leaves perfectly.
I could quietly place a fistful of daisies on the grave.
My fist was the hairy caterpillar sequestering
its poison. But now it is too late. The breakdown
of that story is like the caterpillar, nothing left
but a nutrient soup. And the butterfly!
That metamorphosis was completely out of my control.
The way it forgave everything. The way it learned
to sip its food, and with its colorless wings
reflected everything back as beautiful, bejeweled.

Getting Free

My long-dead ex-husband's wife died this week.
That much I know. What else? She told
no one she was sick, didn't go to the doctor,
finally collapsed more or less alone
into the Bermuda Triangle of her own wishes.
Why would someone want to disappear before she
disappears? I will never know this, either. Things
feel like my fault, my deliberate lack of attention.
        We cast ourselves out of our lives,
there's a crumbling at the edge of what we know,
a bit of satisfaction, as if we'd left shore with its
factories and smells, and climbed the mast.
Nothing in sight but horizon and fresh air.
We take in a breath, a breath made of elemental
parts of a thousand thousand souls we'll never
get rid of, that will be reincarnated into innumerable
more life forms until the sun and earth die a cold
death a few billion years from now.
        But that won't be the end
for those atoms, even the atoms of those
we left with anguish and tears, even those we
turned around in the driveway for, to hear their
pleading to try again. Nearby supernova will shock
and stir the dusty remnants of the solar system
and new solar systems will form around it.
Some of the atoms will make up the bodies
of newborn life forms on the new planets.
Many of my own atoms may have been part of
alien organisms that lived on some long-ago-
destroyed planet. I am sad for them,
the ones who live forever ignored in me,
and the ones who'd longed to get free.

July 20, 1944

While I was being born, the German Resistance failed
    to assassinate Hitler, seven thousand
were arrested, twelve hundred Jews sent on a death march.

Well, not exactly. An approximation. Not exactly "while"
    I was being born. I was slippery. *Cry* and *Don't Cry*
was how I divided things up. In the Philippines that same day,

a coconut from fifteen feet up just missed my father's
    head. He wrote my mother a wildly romantic
letter also describing the water clarity and the fish

he almost caught with his hands. The clarity of his soldier-
    letters, the exaggeration, the childish
exuberance of phrase! Of language overtaking truth

so easily it seems inevitable. Meanwhile, Great-Grandmother
    was slowly dying in the one true featherbed,
Great-Aunt Rhoda rolled her feet on a bottle

in her closet, Nana picked her mums, the maid missed
    the bus and Granddaddy drove her home,
mum until after she got out, when he said, "I don't know how

these people live this way." Events continue to take place
    with dizzy simultaneity. At the cottage, the children
lean over the railing, dizzy with taping Mylar balloons

to the upstairs porch to dangle into the eating porch;
    they tape crepe paper streamers
on the ceiling. They're excited about the cake, the ribbons

they've tied on their presents for me. Which year is this?
    They all wear down into one lump of memory,
one excitement. In 1969, *Apollo 11* planted the first

memory on the moon. And Scott clearly kicked against
        my stomach, although back then maternity dresses
hid the evidence. Always something exciting, even gathered

from view. Especially if gathered from view. Last year
        on this day what was growing in my body
was gathered from view. The excitement has died down,

my head softening with hair, all hopeful again.
        The secretary of state announces resumed peace talks
between Israel and Palestine. A judge has dismissed

a lawsuit between Woody Allen and Faulkner's estate
        for *Midnight in Paris*'s use of Faulkner's line:
"The past is never dead. It's not even the past."

"All of the continents used to be one body. You aren't
        alone." The past still exists in the luminous ether,
and also in Albert Goldbarth's poem, where these other

quoted lines first appeared. They make me tender,
        in a way, toward the mystical—the things
space is full of, and the way we've gathered them into

packages that pretend to come one after the other
        because it's too hard to open them all at once.

Wild

Wildness is before invention: therefore, not
wildness, but simply what is. Invention gave it its name.

When I go for my scan, my body will speak to the machine
in a language that can only be translated.

Meanwhile, the cold and snow go on, twenty below, which is only a
measure
of relative issues, above or below the moment molecules begin to
move into their ice-pattern, though they are always
changing and apparently don't favor one transformation over another.

The wolf is first endangered, then not. During the not, it can be shot.
Who says the wolf is dangerous? Not its cubs.
Ultimately, not the deer, who would overrun the woods and starve
without the sharp culling of the wolf. When danger appears, it is a
perspective.

The cells that were once invading my body were like an engine revved
too high,
all that racket for no good reason, yet they loved themselves and their
neurotic lives.

No perspective is the right one, because of all the others.

An aphorism is always wrong, yet it strikes us as exactly the right way
to say it, succinct, lifting the words in whole phrases, as if the truth
were barbells.
All that grunting to show how hard it is to pull those words
all the way over the head.

If there were snapping wolves below, it would be easy. It's the
 uselessness that gets celebrated.

The scan that shows nothing, that might as well not have been done.
The living that keeps getting carved out of so-called wilderness
and thinks it is special: a carving! a work of art!

Asian Carp

are slipping through, as the lamprey did,
and the zebra mussels, the Irish, the Mexicans,
through holes in the fence, upsetting our delicate
craft, carp huge and leaping, taking jobs
as dance instructors, flinging their scarves
of water, displaying how far even the awkardest
gesture can go,

how their scarves are made of tears,
carp dressed for a blind date with history,
accompanied by circus music, slosh and oompah,
each and each, upward spikes, the neighbor's
radio or their fighting, who can tell?

O world that does not know holy from
unholy, that provides no fabric labels, here is
tender flesh flying headlong into the boat,
here is the breeze carrying even the tiniest
GMOs gently across, an exultation of fittingness:
carp the size of rowboats, dinosaurs exactly
high enough for the branches, pterodactyls
measured for their sky. Then observe the random
irresponsibility of barriers, how our DNA climbs
its own spiral staircase for good or ill, how
the vast interior can turn inside out like a shirt,
how glaciers come and go, the molten lava,
molecular dust, how the hems of the Great Lakes
unravel.

Observe, then, what comes from the pit
of hopelessness and rises on its own like a cork,
springs even an inch or two above the surface
as if with joy, released from what appeared
to be everything but wasn't the half of it.

Grateful

I am grateful for the way colliding and fusing gases
have continued to boil up our sun for 4.6 billion years.
Not "our" sun, but like a stray dog that keeps
coming around, finally called ours.
I am grateful for the leftover orbiting beads of fused
material that became our brothers and sisters, each arid
and silent as a twin who died at birth, always
held tenderly in the mind as the one who might
have understood us.
I am grateful for the Kuiper Belt, where we are able
to keep Pluto and the other outcasts among
its icy flying rocks, to remind us not everything gets in.
I am grateful for the heliosphere, the bubble blown
by the sun that holds its own exactly as far out
as possible, wiser than I ever was, with my soap bubbles.
I am grateful for the stories woven from stars,
and for the delicate brushstrokes of Chinese characters
that leave only the space between stories as if
the dragon, the monkey, the pig, the rooster, the tiger,
are just bones, lit from the inside.
I am grateful for the air inside the solar system's bones,
because this is how it works, how the bellows
are pumped against the few obstructions, the soft
whine, the trumpet, the goshawk, the chickadee,
the roundness of sound itself, as it pushes
through the inconvenient barriers.
Yet I save my greatest gratitude for the slight
misalignments, the outside forces, the variance errors,
that tilt things toward and away, so that I have to endure
the bitter cold only until spring.
Yes, it is the tilt I have to thank for everything,
the sway in your walk, as if you were a teeter-totter
lugging the wash basket down the hall.

Protection

You could almost as easily get a look
at the Holy Ghost as at the box jellyfish,
95 percent water drifting around in 100
percent water, so devoted to the will of
its environment—a virtual flower of Eden—
it doesn't have to have a brain.
It can kill you in four minutes.
Imagine it going from its usual lambency
to flashing along at five feet per second.
You can barely tell it's there, then
you're dead, or scarred for life.
The man and woman across from me
could be on their honeymoon.
They are having a drink and suddenly he
looks through her and is all over
another woman at the end of the bar,
and then he is back, barely a shudder.
Not just the man, but any of us could be
the source of the pain, if we knew more
about it. Even our own bodies hurt
themselves, arthritis and so on.
It is no good reading Job,
because the wreck of his life
has already been explained in the prologue,
God and Satan having separate power issues.
Surfers sometimes wear two pair
of pantyhose to protect themselves
from jellyfish, one pair for the legs,
one for the arms. They cut a hole
in the crotch of the one to go over
the head. Since the stingers are too short

to get through nylon, we may not be looking
for a gross solution. It may be
so delicate we can just close our eyes
and stand around like blind people
until we feel it brush against us.

Cedar Waxwing

The cedar waxwing is waxing and waning
from the cedars and over the lake,
with its oomph and flutter, its long
sword wings, its insurrectionist's black mask.
I could once say "insurrectionist"
with a flourish of hyperbole. I could once
say "mask" and maybe think of Noh,
or Halloween, or hide-and-seek.
Its crest is fiercely blown back,
direct, and joyful in the way of urge, of lust.
It has disguised itself in nondescript brown,
but the blue-gray of sky gradually
overtakes it as if it had hoped to blend there
but couldn't help but turn to this dramatic life.
Viz., the tail has dipped itself in yellow,
either a caution, or some ecstasy
that releases itself at last. Its voice is so thin
and high-pitched it is prophetic. It climbs a ladder
and trills. Even to say the name, *waxwing*,
I have to flutter and stumble. I am overcome
by black face-wrappings, swords. I repeat to myself
from the Psalms, *The voice of the Lord*
breaks the cedars; the Lord breaks
in pieces the cedars of Lebanon.
This is what comes of staying still,
I tell myself. So, look at me, a refugee
like all the others, turned away from the worst
toward God knows what. I have traveled
all these miles while the waxwing is dazzling me

with its aeronautics, its pursuit of the mayfly,
order Ephemeroptera, the insect Albrecht Dürer
included in his engraving, called *The Holy Family
with the Mayfly*, his own mad attempt
to reconcile heaven and earth.

The Poem I Was Going to Write

The poem I was going to write had basic
picturesque snow, but the -*esque*
started worrying me, feeling catchy as
a Facebook post, and then I got overwhelmed
with posts and thought I might wait
until there was enough snow to garner
some hidden meaning. And then I thought
garner was in Keats's "To Autumn,"
and checked, but no, then I spent ten minutes
trying to Google the poem that was creating
my anxiety of influence. Then I had to
shovel, in truth, trying not to mess up
the beauty, not reveal the dead grass
but make a neat path through by spraying
the shovel with silicone so the snow would
slide sibilantly off. I started worrying
about *sibilantly*, feeling self-conscious,
maybe guilty, definitely guilty, since really
it was my husband out there shoveling,
not me, while inside I was basically making
airy nothings. Then I felt guilty for feeling
guilty, a traitor to my craft or art, so I
tried harder to be strong, yet small enough
to fit through the crevices of flakes. Then
crevices of flakes made me wince, hearing
in advance the faint snort of the critic.
And made me feel naked, and suspecting
I used the world *naked* for salacious
purposes. So I put on my hat and scarf and
slipped those small chemical hand warmers
into each glove and took care of the worst
by the curb, to save my husband's back.
The plow pushes the dark ice and globs

of packed snow until they weigh enough
to fall off just in front of our house, and
have to be dug out with a special hoe-like
instrument and then flung upward into
mountainous heaps on either side of our
sidewalk, which is no small task, and explains
why the poem I wrote kept trying to rid itself
of everything else, to get down to itself.

Reading the *Smithsonian* Magazine

Stonehenge, and the recent discoveries using various devices
that can accurately map the underworld without turning one shovel

of dirt. Two long pits superimposed on the photos, a causeway
leading to the henge, those heavy-leaning hunks. How they once

stood, in a perfect circle, great nouns holding hands, balancing
their lintel-stones after much human struggle and death,

welcoming travelers from many miles, we know because of
the bones. *Central as Mecca*, it says here, but I read *Astral as muses*.

The doctor has not yet come in to tell me I am still free of cancer
as far as he can tell. We are outside the henge, we can't get in

to find out what happened or why. It was not about language.
That was me, thinking *nouns*, repeating that old story of stones

walking the earth, of things being better, or purer, elsewhere, where
messages rise from the grass. I thought it was a waiting *for* something,

the rough stones holding their news for eons, concentrating on how
to instruct us while the clouds go whitely by. But now here is the very

white coat of the doctor, towering over as if I dreamed him up.
Either he's a ghost or I am, in my palely flowered skimpy gown,

feet dangling from the table like a child's. I am arms and legs, pulse,
and my secret interior that has said nothing this time, nothing bad.

Surrounded by People

Someone has overwatered the peace lily in the foyer; now
it's yellow and drooping and the leaves have blackened edges.

And people, especially people with sleek sports cars, are parking
in the handicapped spaces. Meanwhile I have been reading

Crime and Punishment, revisiting Raskolnikov in the grip
of his idea (from his reading!) that if one breaks through rules,

he can be Napoleon and triumph over the mundane, so he murders
the vile old pawnbroker (who cares about her?) and her daughter

(accidentally!) with an ax. But no, he's not Superman, he's
wracked with guilt, not that he *cares* for the old woman, or

anyone, it seems, but still, this act is as much degradation as his
(previously unrecognized) soul can bear before he breaks through

to love—for Sonya, the prostitute! This is the basic architecture.
I've poured the excess water from the peace lily, but about

the parking, there's nothing to be done except complain silently.
We're all full of ideas, even the poems have an idea they sometimes

let fly at the end in a white passion, as if it were an ax. Then they
listen for what's out there afterward. Like Raskolnikov, they wait

on the other side of the door, ready for anything, with their prepared
reasons, excuses. Where is the meaning in all this? It's all trying

to Live in some grand way while the actual living was going on—
the novel, the poem, and at the end certainly, nothing more, it's all

done. There's nothing more to say, the page runs out, the effort,
holy or unholy, to see beyond. It's all personality, all these people

living in their apartments, carrying their groceries up in little carts.

I Say Your Name

Sunlight has exploded in the temple of storms,
      of lightning, wind and weather.
    Sun is baring down on the bare earth

in the satellite photo of Palmyra, the flat earth
      of Palmyra, temple of Baal, blank
    space where the temple stood,

where the temple has flown in smoke,
      its weathered yellow limestone,
    its columns, the dignity of ruin, gone. Gone,

the old man, Khaled al-Asaad, the Syrian archaeologist
      who had cherished the ruins
    for fifty years, murdered, his body hung

in the public square. I want to say something exploding,
      but everything escapes like smoke.
    I want to stand before this, I want to be

a column still standing after the torture, the killing,
      the bombing, because there is
    something I need to know, a piece of my being

wracked with dissent. A piece of my being. The 82-
      year-old man, there in the photo,
    crouched proudly before the antique busts, he

the very one who chiseled and lifted them away, carried
      what could be carried, loaded
    what could be saved into trucks, himself

doomed already. I am lifting and carrying the residuals,
      and the sun is taking what it can,
    has always taken what it could, leaving

the rest in shadow. Temple of Baal, Yahweh, false
     god Hadad / Beelzebub,
      these in succession or overlapping, these

to be worshipped or destroyed. These to be
     worshipped *and* destroyed, stone
     by stone dismembered what had been

ardently assembled in the wracking pros
     and cons. Khaled al-Asaad, I repeat
     your name in the name of memory

and its delineation, exact and crumbling as stone,
     what can be seen with the inner
     eye, what can be wholly held in the heart.

Five Moons

Not a bird. Not a tweet or a twiddle. Barn swallows,
bluebirds, western tanagers, probably gone south,
chickadees living on their stash of seeds, huddled
with their friends, fluffed, or in the case of the pileated
woodpecker, in their carved-out tree caves, invisible,
all. This is what the snow tells me: the senses
are always craving, fastidiously revising, burning through
arbitrary places and names. I look at what I scribbled down—
the ragged edges of my dreams.
"FIVE MOONS. NO, BOMBS,"
and now it comes back to me, how some dream person
said, "Look, there are five moons!" and there were,
until they began to whiten and bulge and I saw
they were bombs falling gently as snowflakes,
and I retain that feeling of knowing
the world's almost over, that in a few minutes all
will be white, and I remember feeling protective
of those few minutes, registering as fully as I could,
no matter if there'd be no one to tell. Still,
the crystal-like whiteness deserved remarking,
and such revision as was possible in the meantime.

Mushrooms

It is so damp here it is like an exhaled breath.
The earth has opened its airholes and sent itself up
in the form of little castles, to check out the other side.
Some are bright orange, like small lava bubbles,
one is white with ruffled fringe, and there is a colony
of other bursts, giant popcorn, coated with cedar needles.
Not to mention Indian pipes at attention, blackened
with age. I wouldn't say magic, so easily stumbled over
and broken to bits. They come on strong, then withdraw
as if they've never been. When you get old, you are not
bored with mushrooms. You like to see the bubbling,
which is like a champagne toast. You are interested,
now, in the lively conversation underneath.

IN THE TED KOOSER CONTEMPORARY POETRY SERIES

Darkened Rooms of Summer:
New and Selected Poetry
Jared Carter

Rival Gardens:
New and Selected Poetry
Connie Wanek

The Woods Are On Fire:
New and Selected Poems
Fleda Brown

To order or obtain more information
on these or other University of
Nebraska Press titles, visit
nebraskapress.unl.edu.

OTHER WORKS BY FLEDA BROWN

POETRY

No Need of Sympathy

Loon Cry

Reunion

The Women Who Loved Elvis All Their Lives

Breathing In, Breathing Out

*The Devil's Child**

*The Earliest House**

*Do Not Peel the Birches**

*Fishing with Blood**

MEMOIR

Growing Old in Poetry: Two Poets, Two Lives, with Sydney Lea

Driving with Dvořák: Essays on Memory and Identity

ART BOOK

The Eleusinian Mysteries MS* (poems and images, limited edition), with Norman Sasowsky

EDITED BOOKS

On the Mason-Dixon Line: An Anthology of Contemporary Delaware Writers, with Billie Travalini

*Critical Essays on D. H. Lawrence** with Dennis Jackson

*as Fleda Brown Jackson

CPSIA information can be obtained
at www.ICGtesting.com
Printed in the USA
LVOW08s2244050117
519889LV00002B/206/P